SEVEN STEPS
TO SUCCESS
I LEARNED FROM
HOMELESS PEOPLE

CHET W. SISK

STRATFORD
BOOKS

ISBN: 0-929753-18-6
Seven Steps to Success I Learned From Homeless People
by Chet W. Sisk

Stratford Books, Inc.
Eastern States Office
4303 37th Road North
Arlington, VA 22207

Stratford Books, Inc.
Western States Office
P.O. Box 1371
Provo, UT 84603-1371

www.stratfordbooks.com

Cover design: Vance Hawkins Design

First printing: October 2005

Printed in the United States of America

This book is dedicated to
my grandmother,
Rachel Patterson,
who always
calls me her buddy.

ACKNOWLEDGMENTS

All thanks and acknowledgments are given to my best friend, The Love Supreme, God. I am forever thankful that I lived long enough to have developed the intimate, personal, humorous, and open relationship with God that I always dreamed of but didn't think possible, until I started writing this book and received the revelations through other people's lives, as well as my own.

I also want to acknowledge Michelle. Thank you for being one of my life's great teachers.

Thank you, Mom and Dad, for giving me everything I needed for this moment in existence called "life on Earth."

To my sons, Mario & Malik. Thank you, Mario, for showing me that anyone with heart and conviction can make their life anything they want it to be. You are my hero. Thank you, Malik, for your "indigo child" ways and for constantly challenging all of my assumptions about life, death, space, God, time, and the world. I am making the path straight for you.

Thank you, Grandmother and Grandfather, for always reminding me that wherever I went in the world, I was still your grandchild. And thank you, Grandfather, for laying the groundwork of a life of service.

To my siblings, Denise, Jerome, Wade, and Rodney. A piece of each of you is in me.

A shout out to some of the other great people in my life...

Sister Opalanga Pugh, for checking in with a brother every Friday, even when that brother was AWOL.

Brother Kareem and Sister Maisha I, for the meals, the football games (go Eagles!), the prayers, the washer and dryer, the jokes, the rides.... I asked for a bridge, and there you came.

Brother Thomas Potter, who walked through the valley of the shadows with me and told me one late night"...I think the key to life is making peace with the ground."

Dr. Paul Hamilton, whose intellect is only surpassed by his compassion. Thank you for those stimulating conversations and for allowing me to explore my thoughts.

My sister, Keena, for making me laugh when I wanted to cry.

To the Golden Lady, Karon, for being there and getting my back.

Mahasin, for walking the path few would dare, and letting me take a peek.

Tom and Meagan (Maggie), for creating the triangle of love with me.

Mark, Sue, Dee, and Brad for believing.

To Irene – the early light of the spirit after the dark night of the soul.

My Aunt Ella who gave me "Life Lessons 101."

Reese, for cranking out the hits.

My lifelong pal, Angela, who goes all the way back to those high school marching band days. Thanks for walking through all my life changes with me and providing those phone calls that asked, "What's your responsibility...what's your part?"

My friends and family in Paris, Budapest, Dubai, Amsterdam, London, and other parts of the world. And much love to my new family in South Africa for celebrating me home. *I feel you!*

The people who run the Samaritan House in Denver, Colorado – Father Michael, Della, Jennifer – and all of the wonderful students who passed through my Life Skills class in Denver. Thank you for allowing me to heal and serve at the same time.

My teacher, Mahatma Rama Nand, who always reminds me to go inward.

John Coltrane – for A <u>Love Supreme</u>.

And to all of my friends and family whom I have not mentioned in particular. Thank you for being a part of this path for me. Please know that I love each and every one of you...unconditionally.

ABOUT THE AUTHOR

Writer, keynote speaker, world leadership developer, and international humanitarian, Chet W. Sisk's journey through life has led him to a place of deep commitment to helping others through personal and organizational transformation.

Chet's education includes a BA in Communications from Southern Illinois University at Carbondale and a Fellow with the Walter Kaitz Foundation. This education led him to start his own advertising company, CVO WorldWide. His client list included *USA Today*, JD Edwards, the *Montreal Gazette*, Kaiser Permanente, the *Orlando Sentinel*, and the *Minneapolis Star Tribune*. Chet took a career departure and spent several years as a volunteer at the Samaritan House homeless shelter in

Denver, Colorado. That experience led him to write the book *Making Peace With the Ground: 7 Steps to Success I Learned From Homeless People*. His book provides a radical look at what success is, from the people who have personally experienced the true ups and downs of life.

Chet is lecturing and conducting workshops all around the United States and the world on issues of Compassionate Leadership, Finding Your Purpose, Using Love as a Management Tool, and Redefining Success. Chet's quest is to prepare populations for what he calls "the imminent transformation of our society and the world."

Over the past few years, he has been invited to share his insight at many events, including:

The Academy of Business Administration in Montreux, Switzerland

The Soul in Education Conference in Peitermaritzburg, South Africa

The Interreligious and International Peace Council in Paris, France

The Global New Thought Conference in Los Angeles, California

The Paths to Peace Conference in Budapest, Hungary

The University of Kwazulu-Natal World Leadership Conference in Durban, South Africa

The Annual Conference on Holistic Learning in Toronto, Canada

Chet is also the founder of the 100 Stories to Tell Organization. This organization is dedicated to creating micro-partnerships between U.S. private citizens and charitable causes throughout Africa. Chet works specifically with the international organization Hope Africa of the Anglican Church to help end poverty in rural African villages.

Chet is the father of two sons. He loves spiritual pursuits, cigars, wine and food pairings, old school hip hop, and jazz music.

Seven Steps to Success
to Success
I Learned from
Homeless People

TABLE OF CONTENTS

INTRODUCTION

Ever notice the actions of a child first learning how to walk? She gets up, she falls down, she gets up, and she falls down. The falling down part doesn't become an issue to her until some adult comes along and assigns negative value to falling down ("Oh goodness, are you all right? Poor baby!") Then the child gets the message that falling down is not a good thing. Without the adult putting that value judgment on the situation, the child makes peace with the ground. She instinctively recognizes that falling down is just part of the process of learning how to walk.

But don't blame the adult.

The adult understanding is the way most of us interpret life. There is a general agreement that those times when we fall down serve no purpose except to make our lives miserable from time to time. But the child had it right the first time. The child's natural instincts say both ups and downs are part of the process of learning to walk, and that there is value in both experiences. The only time we adults return to that kind of thinking is when we take some martial arts class or skiing course. In those classes, the first thing we're taught is how to fall, or even more, *how to make peace with the ground.* As any teacher would say, you can't move to the next level of your lesson until you first get *this* lesson. This book is about how I rediscovered the importance of that life lesson through my own falling down experiences and the lives of hundreds of homeless people whom I had the opportunity to spend time with.

The very real and immediate and challenging life situations these homeless people faced brought home the cold hard facts of life imperfect. At least, not in the perfect way many of us assume. Hearing their stories, and taking a good hard look at my own life, led me to reclaim that childhood assumption that *falling down is a good thing.*

This is *not* an expansion on such cliché phrases as "keep your head up" or the ever popular "whatever doesn't kill you makes you stronger." I'm talking about a reevaluation of how we fundamentally look at the valleys in our lives. Instead of seeing them as "bad" times that we'll get through with just a little courage and perseverance, we can now see them as windows to possibilities – opportunities for us to move to a higher level of ourselves. In truth, that's what they really are. They are there to help us learn how to walk.

What I'm talking about is a basic reinterpretation of all our life experiences, both past and present.

After hearing hundreds of stories from people in the most desperate human situations, as well as experiencing some of those desperate human situations myself, I was forced to change a fundamental ideal about life I have held onto since I was a kid. That idea was that "good" things happen to good people and "bad" things happen to bad people.

Life works a lot differently than that.

I'm not a philosophy professor, nor do I play one on television. I come from a place the rest of us everyday kinds of people come from, with all of our warts, shortcomings, and expectations. Here are some other ideas I had to reevaluate:

• If you're good, you'll be rewarded. If you're bad, you will be punished.

• A good education will get you anything you want.

• Life is something to be endured until we get to the end, then we'll be rewarded.

• Millions of people can't be wrong.

• Money can solve most of our problems.

• You're born, you live, and then you die. That's it.

• Tupac and Elvis are still alive.

Any of this sound familiar to you? This conventional wisdom was given to me by a host of authority figures during my youth. It was only when it started to fail me during my adult years that I finally started asking questions.

Now, here are things I noticed in the span of just one week while paying attention to things happening throughout the world.

- A tsunami happens and kills over 300,000 men, women and children.
- A baby is born with a birth defect or dies immediately after birth.
- A millionaire wins the lottery for the second time.
- A young religious girl is kidnapped and raped.
- A hard-working businessman goes bankrupt while several big corporations get millions of dollars in loans.
- A church prays for someone's recovery from health issues and he dies anyway, while someone who isn't prayed for is healed.

Life, as we really experience it, provides us with a variety of events, from great blessings to great difficulties, whether we're good, bad, or indifferent.

Don't get me wrong; there is a fully operational karmatic universal law in place declaring that what you put out comes back to you. But that law doesn't account for *all* of the difficulties and challenges, along with the rewards and blessings, we experience. We usually sign off on the unexplained events by saying, "God moves in mysterious ways."

I think that's a cop out. I submit that God really doesn't move in mysterious ways. *The mystery is for those who just don't know how God really operates.*

In a kind of Jedi mind trick, many of us have been taught that the things we don't like in life happen because we don't have the right hookup with God. What I've discovered is that the things we may not like are just as important to our growth as human beings as are the good times, *if not more so.* Have you ever noticed how much more focused you become when you're in a lot pain or an uncomfortable place?

Here's the bottom line, which I came to understand by listening to the many stories of the homeless people I spent time with, as well as reevaluating my own story:

Good, or an opportunity for good, is in everything that happens to us. It is all determined by how we interpret what's going on.

This book details how I came to this conclusion after spending time in the world of those who lost everything and lived to tell about it.

To some, the title of this book is a bit of an oxymoron. The idea that *homeless* people can teach anybody anything about *success* doesn't seem to make sense. I, too, had to wrap my head around the idea that homeless people could tell me *anything*, let alone guide me to achieve my personal and professional goals. After several years of listening to several-hundred stories, I came to the conclusion that success, as defined by Western popular culture, is not necessarily success but, rather, the definition of someone's life, based on the list of items he has accumulated in his lifetime to date.

True success, as I noticed from the lives of homeless people, is based upon one's ability and courage to evaluate, manage, and find opportunity in the consistent ebbs and flows of the human experience.

Based on this definition, the homeless people I talked with had great insight into success because they were *forced* to evaluate, manage, and search for opportunity in my class. As facilitator, I would find myself helping them through that process by asking them a very fundamental question:

"Is what you're doing now serving you?"

Then, I would follow with an even bolder statement:

"Whatever is showing up in your life right now is a direct result of what you believe deep down inside."

This was often misinterpreted by the class. One student would say, "I didn't believe it was okay for my husband to beat me and throw me out of the house!" Another would say, "I didn't believe, deep down inside, that my wife was going to have a serious medical condition that would bankrupt us and leave us homeless as a result of not having medical insurance."

The response they gave is partially correct. They didn't necessarily believe those things would happen in their lives. They just believed the *interpretation* of those events. They believed those events were terrible and without opportunity, *so that's what those events became for them.* "Stuff" happens in life. But our interpretations of those events determine what they will be for us. I contend that we have been taught to interpret what's happening from places of judgment, shame, guilt, reward, and the ego. Those interpretations can make us miss the greater meaning inside of the event and take us into unwanted and unnecessary misery.

Watching the students go through this rethinking was truly a trip. This book is all about that journey. You, as the reader, can consider yourself a fly on the wall, listening in on the thinking process of people who have seen fire and rain. The wisdom they share – regarding what they did that worked and what they did that didn't work, no matter how it turned out – is the stuff of true success stories.

One of the interesting aspects of homeless people is that many of them are correct and direct. *They have to be.* There is no room for error when you and your family are on the streets. You can't hide your mistakes in next year's annual report. You can't turn your situation over to someone else to handle. It's not just losing the college education savings or capital gains. It's life and death. Their honesty and frankness gave me clearer insight into the challenges most of us face every day but cover up in our "keeping up appearances" efforts.

What I'll share with you are some of these direct and correct stories, decisions, and changes that basically led to a break in a way of thinking for them – and for me. In a very real way, this book is about becoming awake.

Just as the child learning to walk sees falling down as part of the process, you have to be consciously aware of opportunity for your greatness in the middle of a very ugly situation.

If you feel you're not getting satisfactory results from the way you have handled things in a crisis situation up till now, you may want to give this new approach a shot.

You may already be thinking, "How can you say an opportunity for greatness is in a bad situation. Some things are just bad, period." I thought that way for a while, until I put this idea to the ultimate test – slavery in America.

For over 250 years of slavery and another 100 years of Jim Crow/segregation/racism, terrorism was not a 9/11 isolated *event,* but *a way of life for generations of people* in the United States *who both participated in it's support and suffered under it.* The latest numbers gathered by those researching the slave trade estimate between 80 and 100 million Africans died directly from this "peculiar institution." Black people are denying it happened, out of shame. White people are denying it happened, out of guilt, yet, the elephant is still in the living room. How can there be an opportunity for greatness in something as horrific and as divisive as this? How can anyone ever make peace with *this* ground?

When I now look at slavery, I have a different interpretation. This is not revisionist history writing. What happened *did* happen. But what we do with the data from that practice determines what we become today.

In the wisdom of the ancients, the color black was always seen as a power color, unlike the way it has been positioned in modern times, as a negative adjective. In smelting processes, the item is first submerged in fire until it becomes black. When it turns black, you know it has just transformed into something greater than when it went in. I see generations of Black people, African people, leaving me and the rest of the world a message – it is a message of hope and transformation, a testifying that they represent all of us, going through the fires of slavery, changing into a tougher, greater metal, and standing in proxy for all humankind. When we arrive at our crises in life, we can take comfort in the fact that other human beings have become black for the rest of us, and successfully made their hero's journey through the challenge of the Middle Passage.

When we come upon our "dark night of the soul" when all seems lost, we can turn to their example and realize we have the strength and power as human beings to do battle against those personal demons. When we run into those who would have us live in fear, we can draw upon the power of those African souls who faced fear head on and won *even in their passing.*

When we come to those situations where others would try to lock us down, we can turn to spirit and realize that same well of courage runs deep in each and every one of us. Only by looking at the horrors of the Middle Passage did I fully discover the hero in me. Their journey was specifically made for me – for *all* of us. They fell down so that the rest of humanity could learn to walk.

This book is no Pollyanna covering for ugly situations. It is a more realistic look at life from a higher, more powerful place. What I'll share won't be easy to digest. Some of it will run directly against the conventional wisdoms most of us have assumed are irrefutable facts. In fact, some of you may stop reading this book so that you can hold onto your old ideas. After all, those ideas have become your friends, your running buddies, your road dogs, your "peeps." But if you're like the rest of us and you face difficult times in your life, this book is divine intervention.

You're probably wondering, "How did this brother end up hanging out with homeless people in the first place?"

I have a story to tell... .

My Story

For years I lived a very charmed life, filled with success and achievement. Despite battling low levels of depression since my teenage years, I was able to start my own advertising/production company, utilizing the new technology of the time to leapfrog ahead of traditional advertising agencies. I was able to marry the woman of my dreams and take her to places around the world many people only read about. We had two beautiful children, bought our dream home, and made lots of money. It would be easy to take this story down the path of a familiar Hollywood script about the guy who started believing his own hype and forgot how he got there in the first place, then suffered at the hands of his own ego. On the contrary, the more things got better for me, the more I sought my spiritual self and a deeper relationship with God. I never lost touch with who I was. I stayed deeply involved in community activism. This was no front for me.

That's not to say I didn't make my own personal mistakes. It's just that, deep down inside, I knew, somehow, everything would come up to my spirituality. I pursued my spiritual path with fervor, as if my life depended on it.

Then, things changed... .

When the now infamous "dot.com bust" happened, my company went bust with it. The new technology we used to jump ahead of the competition became the scarlet letter to some of our old-line clients, sending a message that we too were arrogant, young, and wasteful. The recession of the early 2000s complicated matters even more. After almost a decade of success, we lost 90% of our client base in one year. Even the champions for us at those Fortune 500 companies were all being fired. I cut staff and everything else I could think of to stop the bleeding, but it didn't help. Let me make a short story even shorter: We lost the building that housed our business; we lost our home, our cars, our savings, *everything*. We faced repossessions, lawsuits, and bankruptcy. My marriage was in trouble. The pressure of our collapsing financial situation, along with growing problems between us, was an intense strain on my wife. I couldn't blame her when she chose to leave me. I came into the marriage with more baggage than La Guardia and more issues than the **New York Times.** My belief was that my intense love for this woman would be enough to heal me. It didn't and *shouldn't* work like that. Healing must come from within. When things were good, it was easy to overlook those skeletons in my closet. I even fronted like they didn't exist. But when things turned ugly, my "stuff" was laid bare. The crisis forced me to finally deal with issues of fear and validation – ghosts that have haunted me since childhood.

Friends no longer called, mainly because they didn't really know what to say to me. Frankly, I also quit calling because I didn't know what to say to *them*. The situation was so dramatic that I was stunned at the swiftness and gravity of the demise.

I went into an emotional tailspin. It seemed as though the harder I prayed, fasted, and meditated, the deeper the problems got. Based on what I knew from my religious upbringing, I assumed God must have been out to get me. Certainly, some of my friends and family thought so. And, as friends and family do, they offered plenty of suggestions regarding what I ought to do to fix the situation. Here are some of them:

"You just need more Jesus."

"Do a fruit and juice fast/detox."

"Quit eating meat."

"You have bad karma from another life."

"Quit smoking those nasty cigars."

"Go back and watch The Matrix again."

"You need to pray more."

"Maybe you should grow locks."

I was *not* going to give up my cigars!

The advice was well meaning and well intentioned (I think). They were only providing information from the place they were in, their space and time. But one friend reminded me of something I had mentioned to him a year before all of this began. At that time, I told him that life was good, but I wondered whether or not I was really being effective in the world. I asked God to make me more effective and deepen my walk. He said, "Be careful what you ask for, you might get it."

Despite my friend reminding me of this foreshadowing, I dropped back into old programmed thinking from my religious background and decided that this *had* to be punishment from God. So, based on the idea that God was mad at me, I started doing things that I believed would get me back into his good graces. I started praying more intensely. I started a yoga and meditation class. I also started volunteering at a homeless shelter, the Samaritan House, as a way to pay penance. I went to the shelter to volunteer as a kitchen worker or as someone who would clean the floors – the classic romantic picture of the broken and contrite man seeking God's forgiveness. But the volunteer coordinator said they weren't looking for kitchen workers as much as they were looking for teachers to run their Life Skills class.

I accepted.

I made a simple lesson plan of classes related to everyday issues like basic budgeting and finding a job. But as my life continued its descent, my experiences started creeping into the classes. I started telling more of my story as a way of bonding with the students. That gave me immediate "street creed" (real-life credibility). That's when they started telling me *their* stories, and the class started to morph into something like an evening of "Spirituality Anonymous." A powerful side effect was that I learned the art of *effective listening*. Even more, it taught me how to tell my own story without shame, analyze my story and the story of others, then provide meaningful and useful insight. In fact, the more stories I heard from my revolving group of students, the more insight I was given. The players in their stories were different, but the essence of the stories was always the same. The more exposure I had to those stories, the deeper my insight became.

That's how I started realizing the obvious – *Everyone has challenges they face in life, but the people who reinterpret those challenges as opportunities experience a greater amount of success and recovery than those who see the challenges as obstacles to avoid, endure, or just get through.*

Working with the homeless also made me see another obvious – if you want people to break from the ranks of homelessness and poverty, don't tell them to change their clothes, *invite them to change their core beliefs.* Dressing someone up, giving them a makeover, or even planting them in a job or home will not end homelessness and poverty. It only delays their return to that state. If they don't see themselves as people truly deserving something better in this life, they will return to the one place that is familiar to them – poverty and homelessness. I know, because several of my students came back to the shelter three to six months after they were released. They heard the words, but their hearts were not changed. I'm getting way ahead of myself here. There's more to come about this later in the book.

Despite these revelations, my personal world had not changed for the better yet. In fact, things got far worse.

Then, after about two months, the miracles began.

I certainly wouldn't claim to be like those faith healer guys on television, but I began to understand how their power worked. People were coming to me each week, thanking me for providing them with a method for dealing with their situations. They were thanking me for helping them get a job, get approval for a mortgage, resolve domestic conflicts, develop a plan for their futures, and for forcing them to see the world differently than ever before.

It may have seemed like I was doing the work, but it truly was them all along. They started to reinterpret what was going on in front of them. They quit believing only their eyes and started believing their hearts. I was just an active observer.

In this book, I list seven particular steps I created from the years of hearing their stories and situations, and the methods that worked for them. At the end of each chapter, you'll see my "What To Do Now" suggestions, presenting basic things each of us can do to activate each step.

Let me also let you know that this is not a book about getting back what you've lost, finding a cosmic way of exacting revenge on someone who wronged you, or a new way of getting rich quick.

It's not that kind of party.

It's just an approach you may not have heard before that, if applied with discipline, can make the biggest difference in your life since you entered the world via the womb.

This book also carefully outlines some of my observations gleaned from years of working with the homeless. Granted, I am not a psychologist, nor am I a lifelong social worker. But I believe my view from the place of a casual observer of the homeless challenge can be very valuable, because it speaks to a perspective, held by many of you reading this book, that somehow the homeless are where they are because they choose it or because they're lazy and don't want to work. There are many initiatives being considered by cities to do something about their homeless population. I believe some of these stories can aid in crafting an initiative that includes a quantum change component. This component is based in the idea that a fundamental change in the way homeless people look at their core beliefs will greatly increase the opportunities to break the homeless lifestyle cycle. I also believe, based on my years of observation, that a quantum change approach can prevent temporary homeless people from falling into the chronic homelessness category.

Just for your info, the names of the people in the stories you're about to read were changed to keep everyone protected.

And, oh yes, this *is* a kind of success/inspirational book, but probably different than the stuff you may have read before. I like to think of this level of inspirational information as "the remix" – similar lyrics to a funkier beat.

Fall down with me.

CHAPTER ONE

REINTERPRET EVERYTHING THAT'S HAPPENING TO YOU.

At the beginning of each Life Skills class I teach at the shelter, I make the announcement that I start from one basic position – good is in everything, every place, and all time. That comforting thought gives me the confidence of knowing that I always walk with power in the world.

I didn't always believe that.

I spent many years of my life thinking that God and I were *cool* but distant. I'm not the only one. An implied, if not stated, idea in the world is that there is some sort of separation between people and God. That concept was verified when I started talking with those in the homeless shelter. I think this was best typified in my conversations with Mary.

Mary was a longtime and faithful Catholic. This Swedish-looking, upper Midwest, heavy-set, middle-aged housewife suddenly found herself divorced, separated from her children, and living on the streets, due to a serious cocaine problem. She was one of the blessed ones, going through a 12-step program and securing room and board at the shelter. One night I asked everyone if they had ever had an experience in which they prayed and prayed and called out to God for supernatural intervention to their problem, and nothing happened. Half of the hands went up, including Mary's: A situation like that happened to me during my "dark night of the soul." I then shared in detail my experience and saw tears of recognition well up in eyes all around the room, especially in Mary's.

I made the bold statement that no matter what is happening to us, it is not because we are being punished for something. I believe that each situation is a door opening, leading to another place of greatness in our lives. Instead of a moment of despair, we are actually standing in a moment of opportunity. I truly believe we are being heard those nights when we walk through the valley of the shadows, and have actually already been provided with the answers we seek. With her handkerchief catching the tears, Mary looked at me with that "how can you say that?" look on her face. I started noticing from that point on that I had a Mary or two or three in each of my classes. They knew what I was talking about when I shared my experience but were convinced that if they just did the right things, they would be forgiven and the hard and difficult times they were facing would soon end.

This may sound a bit clichéd, but I believe in the power of love. Always. I believe we are provided our dark moments for a reason – a greater opportunity for growth spiritually, mentally, and financially. Some would call the tough times "tough love," but I say something else is going down. We are being challenged to rise to another level *of who we think we are.* If we think we are these great beings who can walk through fire and ice with compassion and cool, what better way of finding out for sure than being plopped right in the middle of it.

Those circumstances are also constantly bringing us back to the re-interpretation of what we think is happening to us. Our conventional thought is that the trouble we're facing is a bad thing, but I submit it's a suggestion for us to move forward. If our conception of God is that God doesn't make any mistakes and that we, subsequently, can never be mistakes, then remembering that concept must be the most important thing we ever do in this life.

Let me go further. I have now reached a point of not believing God but knowing God. Belief or faith in God is based on hope that good things will happen if you trust the good. Knowing God is when it's a foregone conclusion that everything that is happening is good. It's like breathing. You don't believe or have faith that you're breathing, you know it. This place allows me to see what's happening to me from another place.

I make peace with the idea that whatever is happening to me is an *opportunity* – not a *punishment*. Punishment makes you want to put distance between you and it and get away as quickly as possible. Opportunity makes you want to dig deeper to find out what's in it for you.

After I shared this thought with the class, I saw hesitation in Mary's eyes. She didn't say anything to me after the first class. She *did* come back for seconds the following week. I was bold enough to share that idea again. Still, Mary didn't say anything to me. But at the end of the third class, Mary came up to me and said, "You've shared some really different things I didn't know how to take. But the more I thought about it, the better it made me feel." She went on to talk about how what I was sharing was consistent with what was actually happening in her life and not with the theory of what *should* happen in her life. The most important thing she said was that seeing opportunity in the "bad" situations freed her from the burden of guilt. She was no longer looking under rocks in her life for some hidden sin and the guilt that accompanied it. She left the shelter with a smile on her face, a vision for what she wanted in her future, and gratitude for being introduced to something that she had never heard before.

That was another common reply shared among those in the class.... I had introduced something they hadn't heard before. A short, blond woman, whose name I never caught, came to me right after class one day, grabbed my hand, looked at me, and then looked down as if embarrassed. I knew she was struggling for words, so I broke the almost full minute of silent handshaking by telling her, "Whatever you have to say, it's good, because it got you to the point of thinking." She then looked up and started putting together bits and pieces of sentences.

"I never heard anything like this before – It's almost too much to take – My mind is just racing – I agree with what you said – I don't know what to do." I knew I was striking a level of resonance with her core understanding. When you hear something that's new and unfamiliar, and find yourself agreeing with it, chances are it's resonating with an inner truth.

The idea that good is in everything that happens to us and that difficult times are opportunities in disguise may be inconsistent with the ideas we all grew up hearing. I believe it's very much a part of our inner understanding.

Just the other day, a hearing impaired, one-time homeless man, Fred, called me about a life situation he faced. He had successfully passed through a 12-step program and had been one of my students in the Life Skills class before securing residence in a trailer park.

He was one of the most diligent students in my class and constantly thanked me for sharing what I had. I didn't expect to hear from him again, so his call was out of the blue. After exchanging our pleasantries, he told me that his trailer had burned to the ground because of a spark that came from a hotplate he was cooking on. He lost everything in the fire, save his hearing guide dog.

After the fire department arrived, he sat down on a rock next to the burned-out hull and pondered the things I had said in class about good, or an opportunity for good, being in everything that happens to us. He said to himself, "Chet doesn't know what he's talkin' about. How can good be in something like this? This is nuts!"

He swore up and down I was talking theory rather than real world stuff.

He held a steady job that paid him a little above minimum wage. He wanted more money, but whenever he asked for a raise, an excuse was usually given by management as to why they couldn't afford to give him more. He reasoned that a steady little something was better than a steady nothing. His co-workers asked why his smile was turned upside down. He told all the fine details of how everything he ever had was lost in the fire, that he had no place to live, and was facing becoming homeless again. His co-workers went right to work. They organized a committee to see what could be done to support one of their own. By the end of that day, Fred had the keys to a brand new apartment in a new development, secured by his boss for a full year. His boss doubled his hourly wage. His co-workers donated money and furniture equaling almost $7,000. One of the workers had an extra car that he didn't drive and simply gave it to Fred.

He *gave* it to him.

Fred said he went to his new apartment and, after those who helped him move had left, started crying like a baby. He realized that none of those things would have taken place had there not been a fire that burned all that he owned to the ground. He said that's when the words I shared rang loud and clear to him, and that's when he called.

I'd be able to end this book right now if all the stories ended like Fred's, but they don't. Some of them happen in an instant, some of them can get quite messy before clarity comes. Some of them are still works in progress. Only *we* know when that "aha" moment comes.

I'd put down money that most of you reading this book, when confronted with a crisis, went down a list of all the things you believe you did wrong that created the situation you're now in. Was it the slight I did on my tax returns back in '87? Was it how I treated my mother over the years? Was it that dog I hit the other week? Certainly, you'll want to take responsibility for the things you've done that have hurt anyone or anything. If you're hung up on the fixes and don't move on to what's the opportunity in this situation, you could miss the new direction that's being presented.

Let the records show that when it comes to confrontations, I take the Michael Jackson approach: I'm a lover, not a fighter. I've been in enough scrapes in my life to know that peace is a much more preferred direction.

I've noticed from being at the shelter that usually people who have been in fights are the last to want to start something. It's usually the guys and gals who haven't experienced that busted nose or the pain of a hand hitting their jaw or having the wind knocked out of them to the point where they can't breath who are the first ones seeking a battle.

This brings to mind my encounter with Leslie. Leslie is a thirty-something, well-groomed, muscular man who told his story of how he had a very well-paying job of 10 years at a telecom company, moving from sales to management. He suddenly found himself unemployed.

He felt the layoff was temporary and that he'd be back at his well-paying job soon. In the meantime, he made the decision to sell drugs to cover his expenses.

He chose poorly.

He was caught and served three years in prison. This man lost everything he ever owned during his incarceration. Once he was released from prison, he struggled to pull himself together, running into major difficulties because of the felony on his record. I'll never forget his words when he said, "I miss my life. I want God to give it back."

I told him and the rest of the class that he couldn't have it back.

That was pretty bold of me, considering he outweighed me by about 100 pounds and looked as if he spent a lot of weight room time during his bid. He could've given me a beat down and not even have broken a sweat.

He now has to move on to a new life, and probably something greater than what he had. Leslie was resentful and angry about what happened and thought it was unfair that *he* had to *give up* his comforts, even though he spent many a night in tears telling God he was sorry. Unfortunately, holding on to what he had was keeping Leslie from moving on to what could be. If he took the position that opportunity was in all that had happened, how would that affect his walk in the world right now?

About the same time I heard Leslie's story, the mortgage company for my home told me that unless I came up with the balance due, I had 14 days to move my family out. Enter stage left, a businessman from West Africa. He asked me if I would be interested in helping him move some cocaine for him. He didn't want me to sell it, just store it in my building's warehouse. "No one would ever know," were his words. He then appealed to my "help the people" side by saying the money from the sales would go directly to the poor in West Africa. That was extremely appealing to me, but even more, he guaranteed that I would earn a minimum of $25,000 a month just by storing it in my warehouse.

When the bank is calling you on a daily basis telling you that they are about to take your building, your firstborn, and everything else you have because you're six months behind on the mortgage, an offer like that can be extremely tempting.

After spending a full day trying to justify it, I reflected on the story I shared with Leslie and how, sometimes, we're presented with signs telling us to leave the old life and quit trying to bring it back from the dead, like Frankenstein's monster. I started realizing, besides the fact that I could never live with myself for doing something that evil, that the situation was really a personal marker for me to move forward. I declined the offer to the West African businessman and lectured him on how he was spreading death to his own people. Even more, I realized that the businessman coming to me was an event exclusively made for me, *right then and there*. I was being told to move on. I lost the building and my home. The high level of personal and spiritual growth that transpired immediately following the losses could never have occurred for me in any other way. For others, it could have. For me, I knew I needed something this dramatic to grab me by the throat and force me to look forward.

One of the most powerful stories I ever heard shared by one of my students was near Christmastime. Her name is Cynthia.

She was a bit disheveled, yet attentive, courteous, well spoken, bright, and by all appearances, at peace. She sat in the front row of the class I taught on the power of breathing. This woman told the frightening story of how she was sexually abused from when she was a young child until she was 12 years old by her uncle and brothers. She said that when she was 12, she experienced a series of breakdowns and spent the next 20 years in and out of several mental institutions. She has not been in an institution for two years, and considers that the great accomplishment of her life. Although Cynthia is coping with basic everyday living skills, she considers her life a success. At the end of her story, everyone in the room sat with their mouths shut, feeling that her story was worthy of a moment of silence. She was worthy of reverence.

At the end of the class, she waited till everyone left and told me how she greatly enjoyed what I shared. I told her that I felt inadequate to say anything to her because of the stripes she's earned in this life. She laughed and said my words brought her comfort and confidence. She then told me how someone at the shelter told her how excited they were it was near Christmas. She laughed again and told me that for her, every day is Christmas.

The way many people feel at Christmas, she has felt every day since she's been out of the hospitals. She now is in her right mind and has found a level of peace. For her, it's all good.

It's hard for us to move to greater places personally and spiritually because it's safer staying where we are. We believe the "devil" is in those difficult times. I never put the devil ahead of the creator in anything.

One of my students seemed to have found a level of peace in his situation that was like no other student's. He was a conservatively dressed, 40-something-year-old psychotherapist who apparently had a nervous breakdown. I checked out his story but couldn't get the details as to what exactly happened and how it led to his homelessness. This doctor, Randle, was familiar with my approach and even knew the language. Sometimes it was like co-teaching with him, for he was able to finish my sentences and was the first to support my analysis to the rest of the class. My approach is not psychoanalysis, but there are some basic truths that I share with the psychology community, like ownership of your stuff, becoming responsible for it, not letting guilt and shame run your life, and so on. After about four sessions, he and I got together for a one-on-one.

> *Me: What's your story Randle? How did you become homeless?*
>
> *Randle: I had a thriving practice, but there were some things I did that were unethical. I won't go into detail, but I will say I made some mistakes.*

Me: And how did that affect your practice?

Randle: Everything just became too hard to handle. Just way too hard.

Me: So what's your plan?

Randle: To be in the moment. I'm learning that just observing what's happening is healing. It makes me pay attention to everything and everyone that I'd usually not observe because I'm preoccupied with all kinds of other things – like bills, patients, and mortgages. There's something to be said about taking a sabbatical. It helps me see things that my everyday thinking wouldn't. This is a kind of forced sabbatical for me, but I've actually obtained more clarity than at any other time in my life. In some ways, the ethics crisis I created was exactly what I needed. I was definitely on a course for meltdown.

Randle's sabbatical in a homeless shelter actually makes some people mad. They resent the fact that he's taking a break from the life we're all experiencing just so he can have insight on living. They think he needs to get back in the race and "man-up" like the rest of us. After all, what would happen if the rest of us took a break from our responsibilities to look for different opportunities that we didn't see before?

What would happen?

We don't *need* desperate situations of trauma and drama to rise to our greater selves, but desperate situations can often produce our greatest selves – *only if we see good and opportunity right in the middle of it.*

Scott was a man after my own heart. He was an advertising executive who worked at a local firm. This 60-year-old man had one of those classic news anchor haircuts with the part on the side. He even wore his clothes in that old school, proper way – button-down collar, high-belted waist, polished shoes. I actually thought he was some highly paid executive who was in the class to assess if his company would contribute to the shelter. Scott had a $100,000-a-year position and was living the good life. A boat, <u>nice</u> cars, a summer home in the mountains, travel, the whole nine. He was engaged to a much younger woman. She was troubled, but loved him. After about a year of being with her, Scott noticed his fiancée became increasingly despondent. Her ability to manage life was slipping away on a daily basis, due to some internal demons few people knew of. One morning, Scott woke up with the love of his life in his arms, dead of an apparent drug overdose.

From that moment, Scott's life took a dramatic turn. He couldn't quite get himself back together after her death. He lost his job, his material things, and his self-esteem. He soon found himself homeless and wandering the Midwest in his car, using it as transportation and a bed. Once he got to Denver, he found himself at the homeless shelter. Here is part of our conversation:

Scott: I loved that woman and just couldn't see life without her. It took me some time.
Me: Where are you now, Scott? How are you working through this?

Scott: The strangest thing in the world is that I actually feel a level of peace and calm I hadn't felt in a long time. Hearing your story – how you lost everything and have come back to teach this class – inspired me, but let me ask you something: Do you ever want to get back all the stuff you lost?

Me: No doubt. I have my moments. I enjoy good living and am enjoying it again. This time I won't let it define me as I did then.

Scott: Now that makes sense to me. I can see that. You know, even though I lost my fiancée in that terrible tragedy, I feel like she died so that I could have my collapse and lose everything – so I could get to this point of understanding what it is I let go.

It's almost like she died so I could see.

Me: Keep moving forward Scott. I will too.

WHAT TO DO NOW

Excluding the situation you find yourself in right now, write down 5 of the unhappiest moments you can remember being in.

In each of those situations, write down 3 things you think the situation gave you that you didn't want. Then, write down 3 things each situation gave you that you would consider a benefit and a plus.

Now for the next week, each day write down one positive thing your life situation is giving you. You may have to dig deep, but you must find something.

Here's another exercise. If you watch television, turn down the noise and just watch the pictures. Pay attention to things that you may not have noticed before.

What this is doing is training yourself to look beyond what we've been trained to do. This is the first step in becoming awake and will help you find things that work and are good. The more you do this, the more you will start to rethink every situation that happens to you in your life, opening the door for blessings and opportunities.

CHAPTER TWO

TAKE A BREAK FROM FRIENDS AND FAMILY FOR A PERIOD OF TIME.

Some of the most consistent experiences I heard the homeless talk about during my work at the shelter were their nasty confrontations with friends and family once they became homeless. Some of those stories made me think of Star Trek.

I am probably the biggest Star Trek fan this side of the Mississippi. However, I do not go to the conventions wearing Spock ears or dressed up like a Klingon Warrior Princess. I DO know almost all of the episodes from the original series, The Next Generation, Deep Space Nine, and Voyager. Does that make me a geek? If it does, I fully embrace my geekiness proudly.

In the Star Trek universe, peace was always being threatened by an intergalactic gangster collective known as The Borg.

These space thugs of cybernetic/genetic origin flew through the universe in a square-shaped spaceship that looked like a prime candidate for MTV's Pimp My Ride. They only had one purpose and one goal – "assimilate" other life forms so that the universe, as we know it, will be one big Borg 'hood. Everyone will be the same. As they say, "resistance is futile."

They remind me of some friends and family members.

The most dramatic stories of abuse, the most intense battles, the most spectacular personal and financial collapses all seemed to center around friends and family members trying to get these homeless people to "clean up their act" or "get themselves together" and get back into the collective. In a sense, friends and family sometime seek to get the homeless to again embrace the conventional wisdom most of us have come to know over the years. Those friends and family members were trying to enforce their will upon these people just like the Borg on the universe. Unfortunately, it had just the opposite effect. It drove these people further away and, in some cases, made their homeless situation worse.

One of my favorite students at the Samaritan House was a young lady by the name of Jessica. She was a 27-year-old woman of Native American heritage from Arizona, who had run into a difficult time. She had been living with a boyfriend who lost his job and then decided to leave her and the apartment they were sharing (which he was paying most of the rent on) and head to Alaska for a new life. After about two months of trying to find a roommate and soliciting friends and family for funds, Jessica ended up homeless. Fortunately, she found her way to the Samaritan House soon after that. The house provided her with several months' of room and board while she worked to get back on her feet.

They suggested that she attend my Life Skills class as a way of jumpstarting her job and apartment search. For several classes she sat in the front row and followed me with a most intense look.

One day she opened up and started talking about the pressure she felt from her family and friends. They told her how much of a "screw-up" she was and that they had told her not to date her old boyfriend in the first place, and that if she had never left Arizona, she wouldn't have found herself in such a situation, and on and on. The tears welled up in her eyes as I heard her talk about the pressure they put on her and her life.

I had heard a story like Jessica's from a woman named Sabrina. I thought about what that young lady did. She quit speaking to her people. Sabrina did it out of anger. She also used some pretty choice words and burned some bridges in the process, but she *did* get those folks to leave her alone. She said coming to the shelter was like a vacation from all the pressure she was under.

Using Sabrina's example, I made the suggestion to Jessica to let her people know that she was out of commission. At least for a little while. I even created a letter for her that would politely but firmly ask them to leave her alone for a period of time, while she got herself together.

She embraced the idea and, over a period of weeks, I saw a lifting on her face. Over several classes, I noticed she became happier, laughed a lot more, and participated in our discussions more frequently.

One day she came to me before class began and told me that she had found a job as well as an apartment, and was about to leave the homeless shelter. She shared with me that the most important time she had spent at the shelter was at the classes, hearing my story and the stories of others and embracing the idea that she was *allowed* to take a break from her friends and family without guilt.

Jessica found a job at a local women's support center. She returned to one of my classes as a guest to formally ask me to speak to some of the women at her center. It was my pleasure and honor.

Ann Marie was another woman who faced the wrath of her family. This quick-tempered Latina had just finished serving a 10-year bid in the state pen, after stabbing her boyfriend. He lived, but she did time for the crime. As soon as she was released, Ann Marie returned to the neighborhood, family, and friends that were a part of that difficult period in her life. In my humble opinion, that was a mistake. For some folks it would be best not to return to the scene of the crime but instead go and make a new start in a new place with new circumstances. But that's just me. I'm just sayin'.

For about four weeks straight, Ann Marie would constantly talk about how her sisters and her children (she had two and they were now teenagers) made her life miserable by telling her how much of a failure she was. They excluded her from family activities and constantly reminded her of the crime she committed. With great detail, she told the class and me of the names they called her, the dirty things they did to annoy her, and the daily mean-mugging she'd get from her own children. When she was first released from prison, she went to stay with her sisters. In three weeks' time, they put her out on the streets. In one class, she asked me the question, "How do I get them to see that I am changed? How do I get them to see that I'm not who I was 10 years ago?" This is how our dialogue went:

Me: *You don't. The new walk to your greatness isn't about getting others to validate you. You are already validated. You were validated when you left your mother's womb. Even before then, you were validated. Every time you look for them to sign off on the new you, you are looking for outside validation of your value and worth in the world.*

Ann Marie: *You just don't know my situation. This is my family!*

Me: *And your point being?...*

Ann Marie: *Maybe you don't have a close relationship with your family, but I have one with mine. Family is everything!*

Me: *And what exactly is your family doing for you right now?*

Ann Marie: *(silence)*

Me: *Ann Marie, I'm not telling you not to value your family; I'm saying you need to value you, too. You can never be*

of service to your family if you don't put you first, right now. Just like the oxygen-mask drill in case of an emergency on a plane, you are first instructed to put the oxygen mask on yourself, and then put it on your child. If you're incapacitated, you can't do anything for anyone else. Let's take the time in this class to put on your oxygen mask so that you're breathing well. Then we can deal with your family members a little later. Remember, it's not about them right now, it's about you. But once it's about you, it will be about them.
Ann Marie: Okay, okay, let me think about that.

Friends and family members often want to reengage us into long-standing and ancient issues because that's how they've come to identify us over the years. We have a tendency to give them exactly what they want. Now is the time to break that cycle.

Based on some of the stories I was told, it seemed as though the friends and family members turned even more hostile, maybe out of embarrassment, when they found that a person they knew was homeless and living on the streets.

But don't hate on them. They're only doing what they believe is the right thing. They're trying to get the person they believe is lost back into the fold. That may make friends and family more comfortable, but it keeps the homeless in the same cycle that got them to the shelter in the first place. That's when I realized that a temporary break from friends and family can be one of the most powerful tools in reestablishing yourself in the world after going through such a major change in your life. It lowers the noise and guilt levels and gives you the ability to hear yourself think as you start asking yourself the most important questions of your life. If you jump back into the collective, you may never take the time or have the opportunity to get the gift that the situation is presenting to you in this moment. I say "gift" because in our society "lesson" has a lot of punitive baggage with it, like "I'm going to teach you a lesson." On the other hand, "gift" means there is a good thing here.

When a life-changing situation occurs, chances are there's something positive for you right in the middle of it. Take the time to get it and don't let anyone, *including the Borg*, rush you and cause you to miss it.

I had the great opportunity to meet a wonderful woman who went only by the name of Sister Carmen. This middle-aged African American woman reminded me very much of the Black women of the church I grew up with. You could tell she spent time in a hand-laying, tongues-speaking, pentecostal holiness church. She knew the phrases, the church "speak," and all the mannerisms of a card-carrying member of the Pastor's Appreciation Committee. I fell in love with her from the start because of how familiar she seemed to me. In the first class, all she did was weep. She wept so hard, I often had to stop my class discussion just to hold her hand for a minute while she regained her composure. She didn't say much that day, but I knew she had a story to tell. The next week, she came to class with a smile on her face and told me, "I've been waiting all week to get to your class again." We were at the beginning of class, during the "testimony" period. In this class, she told her story:

> *Sister Carmen: I have to apologize for crying so much last week, but I had gone through so much, and this was the first place I felt safe enough to just release.*
>
> *Me: It's all good, sister. Tell your story.*
>
> *Sister Carmen: I spent six celibate years waiting for a man I thought I loved to get out of prison. He wrote me every week, telling me of his undying love. I loved and cherished every letter. When he told me his date of release, I planned my whole life around it.*
>
> *I quit working and decided that we would start working together to build his business, as he asked me to. We met on the date of his release and immediately realized that we were not meant to be together. He was nothing like the letters he wrote. I told family and friends about what happened, and the first thing they did was to chastise me for making these kinds of plans. I immediately went into a tailspin and started feeling like a complete fool. I went into a great depression and, without a job, became homeless. That's why I'm here.*
>
> *Me: What exactly did your friends and family say?*
>
> *Sister Carmen: How much of a fool I was. How could I let myself be deceived by this kind of game? How foolish I was, and on and on.*
>
> *Me: And what have you done since then?*
>
> *Sister Carmen: I convinced myself that I must be a fool. I did even more foolish things, which made my situation worse. This was the first time I've allowed myself to really kind of come out from the guilt and shame of it.*

That's what all that crying was about last week. I just let it process through my body.
Me: Sister Carmen, you just keep on walking straight ahead. You're going to be just fine.

Now, before you judge Sister Carmen too harshly, make sure you go back through your own life and think about some of the "questionable" decisions you've made. Of course there's more to explore with her in a "what were you thinking?" session, but my focus at this time was to find out how she responded to the criticism from friends and family. My experience with people in transition is that if the collective tells them how guilty and shameful they are, they tend to seek ways of actualizing that truth. In other words, they tend to live down to the shame and guilt. They never become "better" through that kind of verbal punishment. I expound on this point later in this book, but just know that Sister Carmen's situation is not unique.

Breaking away from the collective can make them uncomfortable because they might be considered a little weird. But that's okay. Sometimes weirdness can be a very cool thing. This is one of those times.

Kenya was a pregnant mom with two teenage children. She had been recently married when her husband of two months started physically beating her.

We're talking about a full-grown man beating a pregnant woman.

He obviously had life lessons to learn and issues to explore, but Kenya decided that she didn't want to be a

casualty in his classroom of life. She left and secured
residency at the Samaritan House. He was arrested and at
this writing is serving time for assault. I spent some time
talking with Kenya about her situation. She would often
talk about how she wanted to rejoin her husband, but
without the violence. She also told me that this was not
the first experience of domestic violence in her life. Two
other relationships with men resulted in physical
violence to her.

Of course I had to get deep in her business and ask
the obvious – "Do you see a pattern here?"

She did. She found herself attracted to men with
issues who usually worked them out in violence on her.
The way our conversation was going initially, she could
have gone back to him without this insight, but this time
we talked in detail about what her choices in men were
saying about her. I am convinced that without this break
from her husband, albeit a legally imposed break, she
could have gone back to the same situation, seeking ways
to make it work without first going inside.

Taking a break from friends and family can be a good
thing.

Another family story I heard was from Luke. This
deeply tanned, leather-faced, stubbled, slightly built,
wiry man was also from Arizona. He and his brother
owned a construction company. He told me that they had
always been friends, but for some reason, something
happened between them. Listening to his conversation, it
sounded like it involved a woman. At a job they were
working on, the two had a physical fight. They decided to

part ways and split the company between them. The split killed the business, and Luke lost everything – his home, his investments, his cars, everything he had. His family felt he was at fault in the fight with his brother, thus he became estranged from him. He started drinking to ease the pain and soon drank himself out of his pain on a nightly basis. The drinking led to homelessness. He has wandered around the American west for the past two years, contemplating suicide and ending up in the mental ward of a hospital here in Denver. He has been released from the hospital but struggles to find his footing.

We often fight with friends and family because, in some ways, they feel we cannot or should not rise above what they've grown to expect from us. They have expectations for us. When we break those expectations, it's like breaking a promise.

Once you realize your temporary break from friends and family may be interpreted as a breaking of a promise, it becomes easier to be sensitive to how they can be offended. Give them time, love, and patience as a kind of parting gift, but do not give in. Do not go back to the old you as a kind of peace offering for the sake of peace. The same thought applies to forgiveness. Don't be too quick to forgive someone or ask for someone's forgiveness. Running to forgiveness can give you amnesia. In your attempt to make everything like it was, you can miss the gift that's being presented to you in the situation. *Sometimes things shouldn't go back to being the way they were.* Everything that's happened to you may be trying to tell you that. I'm not saying giving forgiveness or asking for forgiveness is not appropriate. It just may not be appropriate *right now*.

Susan was a weathered and broken brunette from Denver who had been separated from her family for about a year because of a falling-out with her mother and father. She was determined to make a go of life without their support, and without their drama, but things didn't quite work out that way. She couldn't find work, got involved in selling drugs to support her lifestyle, and quickly became homeless.

Although they were in the same town, her parents refused to provide her with support, according to her, with the idea that she'd break and come back home. In her story, she talked regularly about the anger that she had, specifically toward her mother. She spoke with a lot of bitterness about the relationship. There was nothing I could say to her because I was not qualified to advise her on the subject of anger. I was, however, qualified to talk about the power that can come from stepping away from friends and family for a moment to gather your thoughts and catch a breath. She heard me offer that option and decided that she could trust me on this one suggestion. Two weeks later, she was the first to tell her story of how stepping away from all of the drama in her life actually provided her with the courage to think differently than she had ever thought before.

That was pretty heroic of her. Most of us would not do what she did. In fact, most of the people in class thought the idea of breaking with friends and family was too extreme, and decided, while whatever else I talked about was cool, this was off limits. I respect that. But if you do choose to take this route because the strain between you and them is standing in the way of your greater self, *make your move.*

Samuel was a Black, middle-aged, divorced, long drink of water who looked like he could have been a wise sage in an African village in another life.

He spoke like one as well. Deliberate, methodic, and with measured intensity. He told his story of how his family supported him once they found out he had a drinking challenge. Their support started to dry up once his drinking led to him losing everything he had. He talked of how his family supported his efforts to do something about his drinking, but quit talking with him once they knew he was homeless. "It was like the stigma of homelessness was worse in their eyes than the stigma of being an alcoholic." I asked him how he was coping with this experience. He said, "I wish I had my relationships restored, but I could use a little time off from all of their drama." My experience in this class has taught me that most people's friends and families are working out their own issues through that person's homelessness. A shared perception by a lot of my students is that friends and family feel they have a right to speak to you any way they want because you're not in a position to do anything that would harm them. If you're not in a power position, you can be fair game for their frustration with you. Even more, some see themselves in you and are frightened by the prospect that homelessness can be that close to home. Samuel and I talked after class about how he is handling not having his relationships the way they were. He said: "While I love my people, I am finding more meaningful conversations with these total strangers in the shelter.

"For the first time, I'm actually thinking about what kind of relationships I want during my quest forward. Instead of friends by default, I now get to choose them based on what I want and need."

As I mentioned, many of my friends from the time prior to my financial collapse disappeared. I made peace with that reality and realized that maybe what happened between them and me was right. Sometimes we get frantic about a changing friendship, but let me offer this thought. Sometimes old friendships have to change because they've run their course. Now it's time for new friendships.

No hate. Only love. Things change.

Stepping away from the collective also means stepping away from conventional wisdom, which is that unspoken social contract that keeps you in a "get with the program" lockdown. In this, we are bound to behave by popular society norms and beliefs.

The greatest inventors, writers, authors, philosophers, and creators of our time were people who stepped away from conventional wisdom and the well-meaning opinion of others. This stepping away gave them clarity and a level of courage they wouldn't have gotten otherwise.

A fellow everyone at the shelter called Little John claimed that he had done just that – stepped away from the good opinion of other people; he was a maverick independent thinker. Here's how some of our conversation went:

> Little John: Yeah, I know exactly what you mean. I left those people behind in my old life. They don't want to own me; I don't want to own them. They'll come runnin' to me once I get this business plan launched.
>
> Me: John, it sounds like you're stepping away from the collective on a kind of revenge trip. That sounds more like you're seeking validation than seeking time to clear the air, gather your thoughts, and ask the most important questions of your life.
>
> Little John: No, no, no. I'm just sayin' that once they see me after I get out of here, they'll know they were wrong to dismiss me like they did.
>
> Me: That's my point, John. Why is there a need in you to show them that you're okay now, despite them pulling their relationship from you? It's not about them, it's about you.
>
> Little John: That's exactly what I'm saying. I can now show them how wrong they were in not supporting me during my tough times.
>
> Me: To what end?
>
> Little John: Excuse me?
>
> Me: What do you want them to do once you show them that you're back in the saddle, but this time with a different horse?
>
> Little John: I don't want them to do anything. I just want to show them that they had an opportunity to know me when I was down and out. But once I "blow up" from this business project, they'll see the mistake they made.

Me: For the purpose of?...

*Little John: (long silence) I know what you're trying to say.
I know, I know.*

*Me: Taking a break or stepping back from the collective isn't
a way to continue the madness. It is designed to end it –
or at least take a temporary break from it.*

*In order to break from the powerful influence the
collective has in your life, you may have to spend some
time outside of conventional wisdom just so that you can
hear your own voice.*

*Austin took issue with me about getting wisdom and
insight outside of the very people who brought you up
along the way. He was a 28-year-old dirty blonde who
probably was carded wherever he went because of his
deceptively youthful look. He was a phone bank
supervisor for a collection company who lost his job in
Denver after leaving town to take care of his ailing
grandmother in Salt Lake City, Utah.*

*Austin: My grandmother is the only thing that's been stable
in my life. Why would I want to tell her to buzz off?*

Me: Why would you?

Austin: I mean, that's what you're saying.

*Me: What I'm saying is that if there is ANYTHING in your
life that is trying to get you to go back to a life that you
now claim did not serve you, you should take a look at
that. If grandma is in that category, you should take a
look at her, too.*

*Taking a break from friends and family can help you
discover great tools to help you make better decisions.*

Whatever the case, you'll be able to say, I gave it some thought, and I've come to the conclusion that this works for me, or that this doesn't work for me. But once you make the decision of what you're going to do with that thing or person, you will no longer be able to say it's someone else's fault. Now you own it. You have just taken responsibility for your actions. That's a good thing, though. When you own your stuff, you empower yourself to actually do something about it if you want to change it again.

Austin: *I can dig that.*

After several weeks, Austin and I had another discussion. He maintained his commitment to his grandmother, but he did not go the martyr route. He decided to petition his former boss for reinstatement, under the condition that they provide him with more money, so that he could take care of his grandmother financially, and that they would also provide him with sick leave benefits so he could see her occasionally each quarter. To his surprise, they said yes to both requests. He and I talked further:

Austin: *Thanks for helping me see that opportunity.*

Me: *Thanks, but you know you did all the heavy lifting. I'm glad to see that you had the courage to step away from something and gain better clarity.*

Austin: *But I never took a leave from my grandmother.*

Me: *No, but you were forced into a leave from your work. As I've said, step away from those things that you may feel don't serve you or that work against you or want to keep you in the same place you were in. When it comes to transformation, you have to be bold enough to look at the big picture and be willing to take a break from that which may be hurting you so you can decide what you want to do about it.*

This stepping away or taking a break from friends, family, things, and conventional wisdom doesn't necessarily mean never going back. It only means a temporary change for a season so you can see things from a different place. Should you go back, you'll be different. You'll be stronger. You'll be healthier with a better appreciation of yourself and your friends and family. It is very important that you always show those people love and respect during your break time.

Remember that if someone responds negatively to this change, be patient and show compassion. It's something different for them, too.

WHAT TO DO NOW

Make a list of the people close in your life who may be giving you a difficult time because of the crisis you are currently facing. These should be people who have a great deal of influence on how you think. Write them a very brief letter and send it by snail mail or e-mail tomorrow. The letter should say something like this:

Dear _____,

I would like to thank you for the role you have played in my life to this point. I appreciate what you've given me. In order to build on our relationship, I would like to suggest a temporary break, after which I would contact you at some future point in time. This will allow me the space I need to work on myself as I walk the path of transformation. Thank you for respecting my request.

Sincerely,

This may be difficult for some to appreciate, but you've got to start from some point. Remember, like the Borg, they'll come after you to bring you back into the collective before you get a chance to do your work. Resist, resist, resist!

CHAPTER THREE

CLIMB THROUGH INSTEAD OF LOOK THROUGH THE WINDOW OF OPPORTUNITY.

There is no such thing as a once-in-a-lifetime opportunity. I base this bold statement on solid evidence in the lives of many homeless individuals, and on how life works for the rest of us. You'll agree with me when you take a quick glance of your own life.

Opportunities keep popping up all the time. They often come back repackaged in ways that are sharply different or unrecognizable from the last time you saw them; *but in essence, they really are the same thing.* In the lives of the students in my class, opportunity came as homelessness. That's right, *opportunity in homelessness.* In fact, it's not hard to see homelessness and winning the lottery as two sides of the same coin – they both lead to greater possibilities.

The difference between each window of opportunity is your perception of it. If you win the lottery, the most typical response from most people is that it now presents an opportunity to pay off bills, buy a new house, and get a new ride – all for the purpose of one thing – changing your life into something that you want.

I submit to you that finding yourself in a crisis – like losing your job, being homeless, perhaps a divorce, the death of a loved one, or even a medical challenge – presents the same opportunity to change your life into something you want. Both happenings – the lottery and the crisis – provide an opportunity that makes you focus on changing your life into something you want.

Whereas you are *lured* to change by the millions you win in the lottery, you are *forced* to change by the kick-in-the-butt of being in a crisis.

One way of change is with honey, the other is with vinegar, but they both can lead to a change that apparently *needed* to happen in your life. Again, the two also present the same pitfall. If you don't *see* them as an *opportunity* for change, you could return to the same stuff you had before they came into your life. Take Russell Simmons, for example. I was just reading an article about this founder and CEO of Def Jam Records who said, even with his half-billion-dollar empire, he was experiencing constant sleepless nights, anxiety, and ongoing worry and frustration. It wasn't until he took up yoga and meditation that a change in his view of himself and his world occurred. This gave him the tools to get what so many people in the world are looking for – peace of mind.

The money Simmons made brought him to the window of opportunity. He was able to go through instead of look through that window by obtaining tools that had nothing to do with the money, in his case yoga and meditation.

In your case it could be prayer and daily Bible reading or fasting and studying the Koran. Whatever the case, the situation you find yourself in right now can only take you to the window. It doesn't make any difference if it's half a billion dollars or homelessness. You are at the window.

Catherine was a 20-something single female who left Michigan for Denver searching for a new life from family and economic troubles back home. A lot of her troubles followed her here and she ended up homeless. She was one of the few people who sat in my class and took notes. Session after session she would meticulously write down almost everything I was saying, including my idea that no matter what was happening, an opportunity for good things existed for her, right then and there. Catherine came back to me weeks later and said, "I listened to what you were saying and decided to see how they worked, and they did. I quit feeling sorry for myself and started looking at what my situation was trying to say to me. It made me stop thinking of myself as a victim. Once I did that, I found a job, an apartment I could afford, and a new direction in my life." Sounds kind of like one of those late-night infomercial testimonials, but it's actually what she shared with me.

She "flipped the script" on the situation.

Then there was a 30-something-year-old brother named Kareem who had been homeless due to years of drug abuse, which resulted in his selling drugs to make money, which led to him being convicted and doing an 8-year bid. He was released after two years and then went on to finish a 12-step drug program. He was still very angry about all the tough situations he found himself in. In one of my classes, people were sharing some of their challenges with drugs and alcohol. It was his turn to share. He said, "Yeah, the drugs brought me down, but I have three strikes against me. I'm Black, a former drug user, and a convicted felon. Who is going to hire me?" An older white man in the front row turned around and told Kareem, "Hey man, I was a drug user too, but I had to get on with my life. You can too. Get over it, man."

I had to step in and check both of them.

When Kareem settled on seeing himself as a victim, immediately you knew he was looking *through* the window. Seeing his blackness as a curse is the same as saying, "I can't go through – I can only look through because of an impairment I was born with." That kind of thinking is a direct result of cultural brainwashing. To believe you are less valuable because of who you are is the most profound form of self-hate. In essence, you are saying you are a mistake, *and God did it.*

The drug use and the felony charge were part of a path Kareem must take responsibility for. He doesn't have to make them part of his future, but he needs to acknowledge the part that they've played in his life and what they've led him to. When he declares them as strikes against him, he is making them part of his future, and a negative one at that. *He is looking through the window.*

The older white man in the front row missed one of the important lessons of my classes – everyone's story is a valid story. We all have stories to tell. They are our stories and our experiences, so they are valid simply because we've experienced them. To tell someone to just "get over it" is the same as telling the person his or her story is *not* valid.

Our fight or flight responses will tell us to defend ourselves when someone says our story is not valid because our ego interprets it this way: "If your story is not valid, you are not valid, which means our very existence is being threatened by this person who is telling us to get over it." Fight takes over. We respond with anger, which is what Kareem did.

After regaining order in the class, I went on to tell Kareem that he is standing in front of the window of opportunity right now. When he holds on to being a victim, he tightens the latches that lock the window. He must embrace *all* of his life in order to make peace with it. Embracing is not condoning decisions that he didn't like; it's only acknowledging that they happened. He now takes responsibility for them, knowing that they are part of his life too, whether he likes them or not. To deny those events or see them with shame and guilt only puts a millstone around his neck when he wants to fly. He can't fly with that kind of dead weight hanging over him.

It's important to understand the difference between taking responsibility and being sorry. When you're sorry, you're apologizing. The problem with this is that there is no work being done as to: why you did what you did, where it came from, and what you can do to make sure it doesn't come back in your life again. Taking responsibility forces you to do that work.

I told the older white man that when he does not use compassion, that is, giving people what they really need right now, he too was looking through the window, *but from a condescending perch.*

At this writing, both men are still working through these new ideas.

One barely-out-of-their-teens couple, Hernando and Gwen, came to my class one evening with their six-month-old baby girl.

Gwen listened intently, while Hernando held his head down in what looked like a combination of anger and embarrassment. When he did glance up at me, he gave me that "...man, you don't know how much I really don't want to be here" look. I wasn't mad at him. I really understood. Not being able to take care of your family can make you feel that way.

Gwen explained the series of events that led to them being homeless, from her getting pregnant so young, to Hernando losing his job, and to them being kicked out of her mother's house where they were staying.

Knowing how frustrated Hernando was, I felt I had to suggest something he could wrap his head around. I gave him a nightly exercise to help him. I told him to write down on a piece of paper what he really wanted, no matter how he felt about their current circumstances. I told him to do it right before he went to bed and give his brain a chance to work on it overnight. This is a vision of what life would be like on the other side, after he goes through the window. He laughed at me, crossed his arms and lay back in his chair like a skeptic at a revival meeting when the preacher tells him to come forward and get his blessing. The class ended with Gwen coming up to thank me in a way that suggested an apology for her boyfriend.

A week later, I halfway expected to see Gwen or Hernando. They didn't show. The following week right before class I ran into Hernando in the hallway.

He was smiling and made his way over to talk directly to me. He said, "I just want to thank you for that little 'write down before you go to sleep' thing. It worked for me. My girl said I should try it, so I did for a week. After 10 days, I got a job, *just like the one I wrote down*. I really want to thank you, man!"

A deaf young lady I'll call Beth brought a powerful light to my classes. She came from Idaho after being raped by her stepfather at age 19 at her mother's home. She cut off communications with her mother, brother, and sister after they failed to support her during this tragedy. She came to Denver, looking to start her life from scratch and to get the therapy she knew she needed. After bumping around between friends for several years and losing roommates, she found herself homeless and at the Samaritan House.

She shared her powerful story of losing her hearing when she was one year old, due to meningitis, being classified as retarded by friends because of her deafness, then the rape, then the alienation, then her leaving home with the soul purpose of proving to her family that she was independent and able to survive without them. She and I talked in detail about the last part of this sequence, that is, her desire to demonstrate her independence to her family. This is her window. I told her that the window is not about proving anything to anybody. So many of us spend so much precious energy trying to prove certain things to others. *To prove anything to others first assumes that we are victims and we are trying to prove we are not.*

Victims look through. When you are *a victor,* everything that has happened up to this point is just part of your life path, making you the person you are today. Certainly, there are things we all wish could have happened differently, but the window of opportunity is giving us a chance to move forward into a world we can walk through with love, direction, and power. You could call it a rite of passage, moving from one kind of life to another.

Using the lessons of what happened, we go through the window with a level of confidence and purpose we may not have had before. When I shared this with Beth, she grabbed it as her own. It resonated with her.

After hearing me expound on this point in four classes, Beth came to me with her life plan. It was a well-thought-out paragraph that outlined how she would go to school to become a chef. She would also become the best Catholic she could be. This was a marked difference from the first plan she showed me, where she demonstrated to her family that she could be independent of them. When her plan focused on *them,* she lost sight of *her.*

One of my favorite sayings in class is: "It's not about them, it's about you." But once it becomes about you, *it then becomes about them.* This only means not to focus on others, just focus on you. But once you focus on yourself, you'll find it easy to focus on others.

Walking through this with Beth made me get honest with some of my own challenges from the life I had lead up to that point. Were there some things I wanted to prove to other people, to show them that I wasn't the failure some said I was? Was there some revenge in my heart from those who dropped me off at the bridge when things went wacko?

When my life was imploding, I knew that there was a window out there, and I believed it was in rescuing my rapidly fading company. I did not want to go through that window of change, so I worked even later, spending hours and hours at the office, feeling that if I could just find that angle, that one home run, I could make things right again. I did this to the point of exhaustion, yet things got worse. You can imagine how that "helped" my struggling marriage.

Many people were telling me then that I needed to "let go and let God," but after hearing more and more of the stories from the homeless, the sentence made more sense to me when I repackaged it as "let go of the old, let God show you the new." All of my efforts were directed at trying to regain the old life I had led to this point, when God was trying to get me to consider something new. I finally climbed through that window, but I'd be lying if I said those thoughts of trying to prove I wasn't a failure didn't come back to haunt me from time to time. I now know how to put them in check.

It's a matter of where I put my energy. If the lion's share of my energy is in moving forward into a world of love, greatness, compassion, and power, that's what will set up shop, grow roots and dominate my life. If I'm still giving other people and other situations my power, then that starts to take hold. I can safely say that time has moved me further into the world of love and compassion.

If you ever gave thought to what a stereotypical biker guy looks like, Sanders was it. This 6-foot-2-inch, long-haired, 30-something was tattooed from his forearms to his neck (and probably other places). He had huge earrings, hazel eyes, and a constant "whatever" look on his face. When he first came to the class, he started off in the back, not wanting to be noticed. With each class, he moved closer and closer to the front. He eventually sat in the front row and stayed there. Talk about an intimidating presence – Sanders was no joke. He never batted an eye when watching me. His steely gaze along with his silence intrigued me. I knew I was connecting with him on some level, I just didn't know where. All I did know was that he, along with the rest of the class, was there by his own choosing, so I must have offered him something. After about six weeks, Sanders gave me and the rest of the class some insight into his situation. When I asked if anyone would like to tell the story of why they are at the homeless shelter, Sanders talked about being a former construction worker. No, he did not mention anything about being a biker, but he did say something that caught us all off guard.

In his husky, resonate voice, this man's man said that he became homeless because he felt that he was a "screw-up" all his life. He didn't tell us exactly what that meant, but he was convinced that his life was a disaster because he made dumb choices and did things that hurt other people. He mentioned that his Dad was part of that early molding that may have contributed to his poor decision making. This is how some of our conversation went:

> *Sanders: I don't see any way out of my messed-up life.*
>
> *Me: I'll tell you right now, no one knows the way out but you. No matter what you might think, each of those situations presents the possibility of greatness. Those possibilities keep showing up, sometimes as challenges, sometimes as gifts, sometimes as conflicts. They are all the same thing – that window to the possibility of a greater life. What you might call a messed-up life is really a life with a series of possibilities that keep asking you to choose. You just want to use different criteria in your choosing process, namely questions like "does this serve me?" and "what kind of energy am I attracting if I make this choice?" or "can I live with the consequences of this action?" My job is to keep giving you better tools for this process.*

At this writing, Sanders hasn't spoken again, but he continues to come and sit in the front row, listening with intensity.

In my class, at least an eighth of the students are recent releases from prison. They've served time on everything from manslaughter to theft and aggravated assault. Those discussions and interactions were some of my most dramatic encounters. One of those encounters was with an older Black man who was convicted of second-degree murder. His name is Harvey. Harvey was one of the most vocal members of class, speaking out on a bunch of different subjects, but his discussion became especially intense when we talked about opportunities:

> *Harvey: You mean to tell me that with all the stuff I've gone through in my life, there are still opportunities waiting for me?*
>
> *Me: All I'm saying is that opportunities don't happen on an occasion. They happen all the time. There is no time limit or age limit to when they happen. They are all right in front of us, but only if we see them.*
>
> *Harvey: Then how come I can't find a job right now?*
>
> *Me: Don't get me wrong brother. There are some things you're responsible for that you have to own. There are consequences to our actions and our associations. Some of those consequences may be working in your job search right now. However, that doesn't mean there aren't new opportunities that keep opening up.*
>
> *One of the greatest things about becoming awake is that you start to see stuff that you didn't see before, even though they've been there all the time. You were in one frame of mind that limited your world. Now the window is before you. You can go from one state of mind*

to another state of mind that's probably a lot higher than what you've experienced to date.

Harvey: I don't know, man. This sounds like some of that new age stuff.

Me: Harvey, I want you to take a good look at me. Do I look like one of those airy fairy, Birkenstock wearin', tofu eatin', new age cats?"

Harvey: (laughter) No, you don't!

Me: I'm a football watchin', cigar smokin', red beans and rice eatin' dude who just so happens to be awake. Call it what you want, but seeing opportunity has nothing to do with what kind of religious group or cultural affiliation you have. It's about seeing things for what they really are, opportunities to move toward something greater. You spend enough time giving space to doubt and despair. You're living the results of that steady diet right now. Don't you think you should at least give the same amount of airtime in your brain to hope and opportunity? I mean, don't you think you deserve that?

Harvey: Yes, I do.

Harvey may have seen his life up to this point as one big mess, but one thing I am truly convinced of is that things happen in our lives not as random occurrences, but orchestrated events, grand opportunities we would not otherwise focus on. To me, they are divinely inspired events, leading us to this point – the window.

WHAT TO DO NOW

An easy way to identify a window of opportunity is in a situation that keeps repeating in your life. The particulars may change, but the opportunity for you to take a look at what you've been doing keeps coming up.

Take a good look at your life course for the past year and search for any similar repeated situations. Chances are, those are window moments.

List those opportunities. Then ask if you've looked through or gone through and why. This process will help you identify anything that could be standing in the way of the next level of your greatness.

Chapter Four

Recreate A New Life Vision And Own It.

After you believe you've been beat down over an extended period of time, you reduce life to the lowest common denominator, as a way to make sense of everything. That's what happened to so many of the homeless people I talked to at the shelter. Not to be over dramatic, but when I walked into the room of my classes, I often felt their wounded souls. Some were so wounded they couldn't even look me in the eye. This was especially true of the women who came from abusive relationships. This "looking away" was happening so much, I had to develop a new approach of moving around the classroom when speaking, just to make sure I made occasional eye contact.

But this avoidance goes beyond eye contact. Many of the people were not making contact with their own lives. One of the classes we hold is called "Creating Your Vision," in which we take each student's life and act as though there was no past, only the present and future. Then I ask them, "What kind of life will you create for yourself with the clean slate you've been given?" Many of the students said they had no vision for their lives. Like avoiding eye contact, many of them avoided talking about what life could be for them.

Just as advertising budgets are the first to get chopped by a company during an economic slowdown, vision is the first thing we tend to cut when all hell breaks loose. Our logic is that we have to reallocate all of our resources to day-to-day operations, like paying the bills.

But vision isn't like a Prada purse you get when you want to splurge sometime in the future. Vision is necessary for your soul right now.

Vision requires you to live in the here and now and have a belief for your life's future at the same time. The challenge our class faced was that many students no longer had a belief. Period. If they did, it was deeply buried underneath a pile of brokenhearted disappointment. When I pressed hard enough, I found many people were substituting their religion for their vision.

In other words, their vision for their life was to die and go to heaven.

We talk about the young martyr who is blown to bits in a suicide bombing for the sake of the Jihad, but in reality, we do the exact same thing when our goal in life is to get to heaven at the sacrifice of the life we're in right now. All of the heaven around us is missed.

Some people may think sacrificing life for future reward is noble. I say it's sad. Anytime you forfeit your life right now for some future reward, you're being misled.

Whether that future reward is getting to heaven or hoping for the best for someone else, nothing is worth "being so heavenly bound that you are no earthly good." Many of the homeless in my class all but gave up on what life could be for them. These were also the same people who had a glazed-over, dim look in their eyes. The fire had gone out. The only thing that can light that fire again is vision.

Here are some of the things some students said to me in our first discussions, and here are the translations I gathered from talking with them further.

"I just want a good life for my children."
Translation: "I have no vision of a good life for me."

"I just want to make it to heaven."
Translation: "Life is way too hard for me."

"I just try to take life as it comes."
Translation: "I don't know how to get a life."

"I don't know about anything anymore."
Translation: "I don't know about anything anymore."

"Tupak is still alive!"

Translation: "I just saw another episode of MTV's Behind the Music."

I knew that this class would be very important to those students, especially to those who were only a few weeks away from being released from the shelter. Vision would be one of the tools that could keep them from coming back.

What I did was develop vision time. For 60 to 90 minutes, all we did was spend time allowing people to talk about their visions as elaborately as they wanted. No one knew their vision like *they* did, so I told them to explain it to the rest of us. I pushed each student to better define his vision for himself, because he had to nail it down just to be able to explain it to us. No criticisms or critiques were allowed.

Nothing was out of bounds. Everything was fair game as long as it was legal and would lead them to their own happiness. The more I let the students talk about their visions, the more excited they became. Even the ones who didn't believe they had vision anymore pulled something out of the well. Some of their dreams were old and dusty. I provided them with a safe place to blow off the dust and polish up that naughty boy.

The key was that I created a safe place for them to do that, to recreate that initial joy they had for life – before it was drained out of them by circumstances. Here are some of the visions they shared with me:

• Rupert's vision was to spend a whole year fly-fishing.

• Yolanda's vision was to open her own healing center where people who came from abused backgrounds could be healed.

• Tony's vision was to own his own business so that no one else could ever fire him again.

• Richard wanted to go to all the Rockies' baseball games in a season.

• Barbara wanted her own home so she could put pictures of all her friends and family on the walls.

Then came the second part of the exercise, which involved several key questions:

1. How have all the events in your life helped or hurt your vision?

2. How has your vision changed over the years?

3. How do you think you can reach that vision from this point forward?

These were usually pretty lively discussions that brought out a lot of emotion and energy from everyone. I was getting to something very close and very personal.

At the end of the class, I brought them back to the understanding that whatever is happening in their lives right now, is leading them to the window of opportunity, as we discussed in a previous chapter. What they see when they look through that window is their vision. What they do when they climb through that window is their new life.

Some of this sounded too grand and too fantastic for some of the students, but the alternative was that they would have to continue to shrink their lives down to a place of least expectations.

You may not be homeless, but you may be thinking like a homeless person – you want to do just enough to get by so you can just get to the finish line. You consider life something to be endured. Your expectations don't go beyond this week's paycheck. Your world has been reduced to three squares and a television remote. As I discovered with my class, bringing back your vision has a way of igniting the soul to levels of courage we may have thought we didn't have.

Some of the students said they had more immediate stuff to take care of, so vision would have to wait. I then introduced them to breaking vision down into increments. If it's too hard seeing what's going to be up next year, break the vision down into three-month increments. What do you want your world to look like then? Six months from now? Nine months from now? Breaking down your vision into smaller portions actually provides a more realistic step-by-step approach for dealing with life events we don't expect or anticipate.

When we make peace with the ground, vision is that force that drives us to rise from that place so we don't get too comfortable down there.

It took a lot of work for me to recreate my own personal vision of life. So much of what I had known up to this point had been changed. A year before things started falling apart, my father died of cancer, at the age of 64. His passing forced me to rethink the world as I knew it and cast a new vision of going forward. The world was a different place with him not in it, as he had been for all my life. His passing was like a warning shot of even more personal changes I would soon experience. A year after he passed and a week after the bankruptcy of my business, I woke up and asked myself, "What is life all about?" These changes, along with knowing my father wasn't here anymore, gave me a deep sense of emptiness I couldn't quite explain. I knew I had to create a new vision for my personal survival as well as that of my family, but I guess I just didn't want to at that time. I knew I couldn't stay in this land of limbo too long. People depended on me. Creating a new vision to walk through the series of crises I faced was like chasing after my next breath – without that next breath, I would die.

Knowing the seriousness of the situation, I created a formal routine that would press me toward vision creation. Each morning for about two months, the first thing I would ask myself when I opened my eyes from sleep was, "Who am I?" This made me focus on the idea that I am connected to God, the universal source for everything, and there is no separation. I would follow this with time spent in meditation, just to clear out any worries and anxieties.

Then, I daydreamed. While riding the bus on my way to work, I let my mind wander wherever it wanted to go. This lead to some rich ideas about what was possible in the next part of my life. Finally, I would surround myself with people who had a vision for their own lives, and I would talk with them on a regular basis. These people encouraged me to articulate and share my vision. They didn't judge me. They wanted me to know that they provided a safe place for me to explore my thoughts and express them out loud.

It could be said that Phillip was the court jester of the class. This 28-year-old African American man always had a smile on his face, a sparkle in his eye, and something smart to say about anything and everything. He told me that he enjoyed my class immensely, but I suspect that it wasn't only because of the deft knowledge that was being shared by the students and myself, but because the class gave him a platform to have a field day when expressing his views and insights. Many of those ideas had great merit and were perfectly on time when it came to addressing a particular situation. But more often than not, Phillip was frontin' – he just wanted to hear himself talk and make sure others heard him talk, too. But that's just me observing what I saw. Most of the time, his insight was keen and dead on. Here is one of our exchanges about vision:

> *Phillip: What's the difference between what you call vision and remote viewing.*
> *Me: You know about remote viewing?*
> *Phillip: I know that the CIA ran a remote viewing program for almost 50 years here in the U.S.*
> *Me: I'm impressed that you know that. And no, for the record, remote viewing is not the vision that I'm talking about. The mistake we tend to make is that we believe only people with special positions in life have vision – the CEO who has a vision for his company, the preacher who claims to receive visions from God, the artist who has*

vision for a painting. Truth is, we all have a vision we can aspire to. It doesn't have to be some grand, glorious whiz-bang thing. It can be as simple as learning how to read or becoming a chef at a restaurant. If it is something we want to do, it can become our vision.

Phillip: Well I don't think I have vision. I mean, the only thing I think about is women. Is that my vision?

Me: What, to have one or to be one?

Phillip: (laughter) No, to have one – or more.

Me: Just checkin', my friend. If you want to be one, there are operations that can get the job done.

Phillip: (laughter) No, to have one or two.

Me: Then you need to define it more specifically so that when you set your vision in motion, you're being quite clear about what your intention is. If you are ambiguous about what your vision is, it will eventually show up ambiguously in your life. The universe doesn't judge. It just responds to what you put out.

Phillip: You know, that's kind of what homelessness feels like to me. A kind of ambiguous life, you know what I mean?

Me: Break it down for me... .

Phillip: I mean, you move from one state of existence to another, not quite sure what's going to happen next. Shelter to shelter, meal to meal. Hoping for one thing and seeing somethin' else. You never get a chance to just chill for a minute because you're always in motion, hoping for the next situation to be cooler than the last one.

Me: So does that mean you can't have a bigger vision for your life?

Phillip: No, but when you're trying to survive, that becomes your vision... .

Me: And your self-fulfilling prophecy. I'm not mad at you for doing the survival thing. I'm just saying that until you start having a bigger vision for your life, more than just day-to-day, that's all you'll ever have. And no one in the world will be able to change that but you.

Phillip: Well that's all cool coming from a college-educated dude like you, but how do us ordinary people get vision?

Me: Don't try to make this into some kind of class thing, Phillip. You've got the power of vision, too. It's just been buried for some time underneath all your survival mode stuff. Make no mistake. Vision is survival mode stuff, too. Like the scripture says – without vision, the people perish.

My time at the shelter made me realize that everyone can have a vision for their lives, as long as we don't paint the idea as some grand concept for people who have their lives in order. I believe the greatest visions come when we're catching the most amount of grief in our lives. That means broken people can recreate a vision for themselves that can move them forward, through the window of opportunity. That vision creates life, hope, and a peace with the ground.

WHAT TO DO NOW

Gather only your closest and most trusted friends and family members, break out your favorite beverages, music, and food, and have a "Vision Party." This is where you share your vision with people who will only support and empower you. You'll know who they are.

There are only two rules in a gathering like this:

1. No one is allowed to criticize your vision. It is your vision. Because it is your vision, it is inherently valuable. As I mentioned at the start of this book, everyone's experience is valid. That means everyone's vision is valid.

2. Whatever you share at the party stays at the party.

Some people disagree with you sharing your vision, feeling that it could take some energy away from its manifestation. However, based on my experience with the homeless, sharing your vision only empowers you.

CHAPTER FIVE

GET A SPIRITUAL BUDDY TO WALK THROUGH YOUR LIFE'S CHANGES WITH YOU.

After one of the classes at the homeless shelter, an appreciative student came up to me and said, "You're my guru!"

When I was growing up, gurus were considered wack dudes who pimped other people so that they could have their pick of luxury cars and women.

I felt this way until I finally found out the term guru actually means teacher. If that's the case, I've had gurus since kindergarten. In fact, I even fell in love with a substitute guru I had in the fifth grade, because she looked like Lieutenant Uhuru from the original Star Trek series.

I was one of the lucky ones during my crisis. The universe saw fit to send me a number of gurus. One of them is my yoga and meditation leader. This sage from India is a man of uncommon wisdom and spiritual truth.

We would sometimes take walking meditations and nature walk classes that allowed me to ask tons of questions when I was going through my toughest days. He is the one who made me recognize the difference between knowing *of* God as opposed to knowing God. When I owned my building, my maintenance man was a profound guru who shared real-life insight from his own experiences. This man served several years in prison for assault but managed to live through those years by regularly reading the Bible and the works of the Sufi poet Kahil Gibran. Another sister-friend of mine, an African storyteller, called me regularly on Fridays just to check in with me to see if I was doing okay and to occasionally share a classic West African story, as well as some of her own life adventures, for context.

The power of the guru, spiritual coach, and spiritual buddy is greatest when they do not tell you what to do. They are only there to share some of their experiences and witness your experience with you, then direct you back to yourself so that you can hear that still small voice. It's good for them to provide you with methods of coping with the situation, but the methods, again, should always lead you back to the answer given to you from your inner knowing.

The idea of having a guru or witness was completely foreign to those at the shelter. Sure, they had plenty of people who were willing to tell them what to do to make their situation go away.

The danger here is that making your situation go away keeps you from finding the gift right in the middle of the situation. One young lady named Tia, a Latina from Las Vegas, talked about how her minister chastised her about her homeless situation (caused by abuse in her home by her boyfriend) and ran down a laundry list of do's and don'ts.

An older woman, Helen, said she went to her minister for help and advice in her situation, but didn't get either from him. I imagine that she didn't get what she asked for because the sheer number of people he has to tend to overwhelmed him. Remember, don't hate on others if they can't help you right now. Your path is still leading you to great things. You just may have to find your "gurus" in nontraditional places. I told Helen that the reason she didn't get what she wanted from the minister may have been that she was being asked to look internally for the same things. In another one of those miracles, she came back to me the next week and let me know about a whole list of new things she could do for herself. Those things weren't hidden from her. She just never saw them in herself when her eyes were fixed on the minister.

A very vocal and contentious young guy from Denver named Pete asked me if I was saying that they should not go to church for guidance. Let me say this about that subject. Most of the major religions were represented in my classes at the homeless shelter. I personally believe there is a difference between religion and spirituality.

Religion usually represents a formal institution. Spirituality represents a personal relationship. I feel that spirituality is the key to everything and that the guru should direct the student to developing that relationship.

But I digress.

The walk you are on is an individual one. At the same time, without support from the guru or spiritual buddy, it is easy to lose your way. With me playing the role of the spiritual buddy or witness, the class gave each person there a chance to do the self-exploration most people don't do in a lifetime. It created a safe place where spirituality and inner searching was not something restricted to philosophers, clergy, and college students, but something every person needs to do. It's the only place where an idea like making peace with the ground will get a chance to sink into your consciousness.

In every one of my classes, at least 15 percent of the students were veterans. Sam was one of them. This 45-year-old served in the Gulf War. He ended up in the homeless shelter because he just simply wasn't able to adjust to life since coming back. He had a family before the war, but his erratic behavior after returning created intense strife between him and his wife. They separated and he ended up homeless, trying to find himself. Sam came from a Pentecostal background, which gave him a very definitive way of looking at the world.

He was comfortable with that view and initially suggested to me that I really couldn't tell him anything he didn't already know. He regularly attended my class, initially out of curiosity, then out of frustration, because I included teachings from wise men and women outside of the Pentecostal tradition.

He challenged me on my information and questioned my facts. I shared with him what I knew and invited him to check my facts out for himself. The teacher always directs the students back to themselves so that they will do the work.

After several challenging and sometimes contentious classes with Sam, there was a change. Sam talked less and started taking pages and pages of notes about everything I said.

After one class, I asked Sam how things were going. He looked at me, smiled, shook my hand, and thanked me for making him do the work of going from a belief system to a knowing. A belief is what we've been taught to know. A believer in this system seeks evidence or proof for what they think is true, requiring regular convincing. A knowing is when you accept an idea as truth, without the need of proof or evidence. It is an inner knowledge that is assumed with complete confidence. Breathing is a knowing. You don't stop to think about it, you just assume its truth on a greater understanding. Just like breathing, knowing is an inner knowledge inside each and every one of us. The job of the teacher is to direct the student back to that inner knowing.

I also had the privilege of meeting Tom. Tom was a thin wisp of a man who looked like he could be a professional college student, if you know what I mean. He hated that I often used the term "God" because he was Agnostic (which literally means – choosing not to know). So, I started interchanging the word God with love, spirit, and good. In my mind, they are all the same thing, and I believe in being flexible. I did not, however, change the essence of my approach. I believe in the Thelonious Monk method.

Thelonious Monk was a jazz pianist who faced intense criticism from so-called jazz critics for many years. That never stopped him from continuing his work, tirelessly and relentlessly. Years later, Monk was called a pioneer, ahead of his time, a ground-breaking musician who had a vision of where jazz was going – a complete about face. Some of this was coming from the same critics who hated on him the first time. But Monk was never rattled. He just kept doing what he did best – playing his style of jazz.

As a teacher, I'm to bring the lesson, as it is clear to me. That's my job – stay focused on the task, put out the intention, and release myself from the outcome, or how it is received. I tell the students that I come to class to bring a lesson, *drop it like it's hot,* then move on.

Several weeks later, Tom came to me after class and asked me to be his personal spiritual teacher. I was stunned and asked him what brought about this change of heart. He said it wasn't a change of heart as much as it was him seeing how consistent I was about what I believed and that I never judged anyone, no matter where they were or what they said. Though flattered by his request, I respectfully declined. I keep a very rigid line between my work at the shelter and doing any work with those same people outside of the shelter. This allows me to focus on my task then and there and make room for the next teacher to come into their lives.

Before you trust someone in this important position in your life, as you walk through the valley of the shadows, you should ask these questions:

• What kind of experiences have they had? My gurus have always been older, simply because they've seen more of life than I have.

• What is their core belief system? It is best to find someone who will define to you what their core belief system is up front, and hopefully one who appreciates the thousands of religions and beliefs that exist in the world today.

• What is their availability like? Can you reach them during crucial times without taking advantage of their time, too?

• What is their prayer and meditation life like? There is no right or wrong answer to this. It's just something you should know so that you understand what to expect from them.

Remember, the goal of the spiritual guru or buddy is not to make you dependent on them, but rather to have someone help you develop your own spirituality so you can start trusting that still small voice inside of you.

That's what I dig about my teacher. I'd ask a question, and he'd say something like "meditate on it" or "what do you think?" or "the answer will come to you." At first, that was extremely frustrating. With everything going on around me, I wanted a quick fix. But what he was doing was laying the groundwork for me to go inside. At our gatherings, he never passes a basket for donations, never requires a dress code, or has me and the others sign membership cards. In fact, he told us that eventually he'll have to kick us out of his class so that we'll make our way in the world with our newfound understanding. He's not building an institution, dependency, or a following. He's just giving us the tools we need to walk differently in the world. To me, that makes sense.

There was a 40-something-year-old man who had all of his teeth knocked out because of some drug feuds he had been involved in. He reminded me of the great trumpeter Chet Baker in his latter days. In fact, his story of why he lost his teeth is almost identical to Baker's. This guy named Nero immediately recognized my approach and the language that I used about transformation. We became involved in a serious discussion right in the middle of one class:

> Nero: *I know exactly what you're talking about. It sounds very Gnostic.*
> Me: *Well Nero, don't hold all the knowledge to yourself, share with the rest of the class.*
> Nero: *Well, as you probably know, the Gnostics were the original Christians who understood the faith from the place that the light of God is in each and every one of us, and all we have to do is wake up to that fact. Once we do that, our lives will change and transform into something great.*
> Me: *Pretty heady stuff, Nero. Where did you get that information from?*

Nero: After my near-death experience of being beaten unconscious by some dudes robbing me of my teeth and my drug money, I was introduced to a Gnostic teacher out East who told me some really deep things.

It was those teachings that first allowed me to start to turn my life around. Once I knew I had the light, too, I could finally start to see the world and my life from a different place. He walked with me through my dark night of the soul. You were right when you said they shouldn't get in the way. All my teacher did was come to the hospital, hold my hand, and keep telling me to dig deep for the meaning. What you're saying is so familiar.

Me: Do you still have that teacher in your life?

Nero: Not like I did back then. I had learned all that he could give me. He sent me on my way and said that I would meet new teachers as I continue to grow. Apparently, you're one of those new teachers.

Me: Of course, you know those dudes who knocked your teeth out were your teachers, too.

Nero: You got that right. I didn't see them that way at first because the pain kind of preoccupied my thinking, but you're right.

My belief is that the job of the teacher is to eliminate her own job. The teacher is there to create more teachers, not more students. My guru was adamant about that.

His teaching helped me understand and get grounded in the idea of unconditional love and compassion, *no exceptions.* I guess the old saying is right, when the student is ready, the teacher will appear – just in time to help me make peace with the ground.

WHAT TO DO NOW

Use the criteria provided earlier in this chapter to find someone who can be your support. Schedule time with him or her on a regular basis, just to share your experiences. Remember, these people don't have it all worked out. They have challenges they are working through, too. They are only there to witness – letting you know three primary things:

1. You are not alone.
2. You are loved.
3. You will get through these tough times.

Don't be discouraged if you cannot identify this person immediately. Have patience and take your time. As I mentioned earlier, when the student is ready, the teacher, or witness, will appear.

CHAPTER SIX

QUIT WATCHING TELEVISION FOR A THREE-MONTH PERIOD.

You've heard me mention "noise" throughout this book. I feel very strongly that noise is what keeps most people dazed and confused when navigating through their greatest challenges. That was so obvious with the homeless people I worked with; it was criminal they didn't notice it before. Take a good look around you. Almost everything around you is vying for your attention and trying to give you a message.

I noticed from listening to my students that the homeless lifestyle is a very noisy lifestyle. The idea of contemplative thought and quiet time seems to be something that the homeless are robbed of. Whether it's by the constant moving around from place to place or the noise created by a system seeking to place homeless people into jobs or homes, they are constantly being bombarded by high levels of noise and the tension that it brings. Even on a personal level, there is a never-ending chorus of voices and noises that tend to distract and confuse. From friends and family telling them what to do, to the escapism of television so that they don't have to cope with the day-to-day challenges of an inner voice of guilt and shame fed by society, the beat goes on.

Homelessness is a very dense state of being. It is for this very reason that I shared with the class the most effective thing they can do to give themselves a fighting chance at sanity.

Most of us who are not homeless actually have many opportunities to create peace and quiet; it's just that we almost automatically seek to fill that silence with noise.

Find out where you are. Answer these test questions:

• When you come home from work, is turning on the television or stereo the first thing you do so that you can have "company"?

• When you're talking to someone and there is a big gap of silence, do you seek to fill it because the silence makes you uncomfortable?

• When alone and by yourself, do you start to imagine that you're part of a horror movie and some weird dude will come from behind the door and bite you on the neck?

If you said yes to just one of these test questions, you're afraid of silence. If you said yes to that *last* test question, you're *definitely* watching too much television.

George was an older working-class man. I believe he was of first generation German descent because of his distinct and heavy German accent. He originally asked to be excused from my class. I told him that this class was not mandatory, so if he wanted to leave, he could. He must have thought I was trying to put some reverse psychology on him because he sat down and decided to stay. I meant what I said, but I was glad he stayed, just the same.

I began the class talking about the power of silence and solitude so that one has the chance to hear himself think and become fully conscious of the moment. George never said a word, but when I started digging deeper about how important it is to have daily silence and give yourself a chance to hear yourself think, his face changed dramatically. He went from staring at walls and other parts of the room to an intense gaze at me. I didn't think I was saying anything exceptionally remarkable in that class. Perhaps, that day, I must have been pushing his buttons. His look started off as defensive and a bit condescending and changed to fragile and vulnerable. I knew this subject was cutting like a hot knife through butter. I felt him almost reach out and grab me, spiritually. I said to the class, "Your thoughts and ideas have meaning and worth. Don't you think they deserve a little consideration from you? Give them what they need – attention.

The only way you can give that to them is by lowering the noise." At the end of the class, George greeted me with a weightlifter's grip. He looked at me with deep, tear-filled eyes. He didn't say anything, but he didn't have to. I knew he came from a generation where sharing your emotions was a sign of weakness. He was kind of like my Dad. He expected me to get what he meant without a whole lot of words. I did get it. I gave George his props with a nod and a firm grip back.

George did make me think more about the things my Dad left me, but I had to get past the noise of my Dad's loss. The noise of seeing the cancer beat down on my Dad's body haunted my night dreams and daydreams for more than a year. In our home, we had a prayer room. This room allowed me to sit in complete silence late at night, meditating, praying, and thinking. That's where the gifts from my Dad started to unfold. I finally came to the understanding of all the things he had left for me, even in his passing. Here are some of them:

• I did not lose my Dad. In many ways, our spiritual relationship is deeper than the one we could ever have had while he was here on earth. I actually *gained* my Dad.

• He left me with a powerful work ethic that functioned, even in my darkest hour. I never saw him miss a day of getting up and going to work. No matter what was happening in my world during my crisis, I saw myself as my Dad, getting up and going to work.

• He made me look closer at my relationship with my own two sons. My relationship with my Dad was warm, but distant. That's just how it worked with his generation, and probably the generation before his. His death refocused my attention on breaking that cycle and making sure my boys would always hear from me the words "I love you." I want them to always see that love in action.

• My Dad's drive for achievement became my drive for achievement. For years I thought it was just something I developed on my own. Shutting down the noise allowed me to remember key things he said and did that I now find myself mirroring. He gave me those things, along with being timely, courteous, and becoming an entrepreneur.

• My Dad's passing made me refocus on the beauty of my Mom. I know their relationship had its ups and downs like all relationships. There were some particular incidences in their lives that challenged them beyond what most people know. Even with those challenges, it was my Mom who took care of my Dad without hesitation during those long and dark walks through the valley of cancer. She told me how tough it was. She never backed away from what she had to do. When I went back to my hometown to spend the last few days with my father before his passing, I fully realized the enormity of all she had to do for him, as he was not able to take care of himself. My Mom is a Saint.

I like to think of my Dad's life as a spectacular firework display. He was a lit rocket powering up to the sky. At his passing, the firework exploded into a kaleidoscope of brilliant colors and fantastic pyrotechnic design. All I had to do was open my eyes and see.

Turning down the noise and turning off the junk involves more than creating moments of silence. It also involves your personal media. It is the stuff in your life that gives you little messages throughout your day. Check out some of the messages on the T-shirts my students were coming into class with:

"Life's a B—— And Then You Die"
"I'm With Stupid"
"Don't Mess With Me, I'm Having A Bad Day"
"Let's All Get Drunk"

I'm just guessing here, but could there be some relationship between some of my student's personal media and the challenges in their lives? I'm just sayin'...

I asked the students to go to their rooms, look around, and see what kind of messages they may be telling themselves on a daily basis. From their coffee cups to paintings and posters, to magazines, books, tapes and CDs, I asked them to take a look at everything and see what messages they were sending themselves every waking moment of their lives. I say that if the noise and the junk do not support the idea that you are a wonderful person made in the likeness and image of the Creator, you need to question why you have it. That's the same with the stuff in your car, especially the music you listen to.

If it's talking about destruction, cheating, violence, and disaster, it's probably working against you. Yes, we all like the banging beat, but don't be mislead, your brain is a steel trap – it doesn't miss a thing, especially the spoken word. Whatever the singer or rapper is saying, your brain takes it in and stores it as reference to be used at some future date.

Dillon was a very anxious, intense, 35-year-old dyed platinum blond man from Missouri who was quite troubled. He would come to my class and was hardly able to sit still, as his anxiety seemed to get the best of him.

He would often interrupt my discussions with dramatic disagreements. When I talked about creating a place of silence so you can hear yourself think, he told the whole class that what I talked about was silly. After one class, I asked him what was eating him. He told me about how he was dogged out by his former roommates.

He became homeless when they decided to put him out because they just didn't like him anymore. I asked him how that made him feel. He said each day he woke up with hate in his heart for them. He said he often spoke of hurting them physically and destroying their lives through violence. I asked him how often he thought of this. He replied – all the time. I invited him to participate in a burning ceremony. In this ceremony, we all wrote down things that were no longer serving us, then put them into a big bonfire, symbolically telling ourselves that those things were no longer part of our lives. Dillon participated. He wrote down and burned his hate, but told me he still was not satisfied. I suggested that he take a long walk in the city park as part of a walking meditation. No music through headphones, no discussions with others, nothing. I asked him to experience the silence of walking and observing, every day for a week.

After that week, Dillon actually manifested a welcomed level of peace in my class. He quit talking so much and sat in the front row at attention. I knew the walking meditation was having an impact. He confirmed it, and shared that the more he meditated, the more peace he had. This might seem elementary to some of us, but to Dillon it was revolutionary. All Dillon did was turn down the noise and allow himself to go beyond the hate to re-establish the peace he already had inside.

It doesn't take a scholar from the University of Timbuktu to realize our society is not designed for people to experience interpersonal silence and contemplation. On the contrary, it's designed to make you pursue more noise in an effort to influence your behavior. As a media consultant and radio personality, I can tell you about one of the industry's little secrets. The first few times you hear a song on the radio, you may like it, but will not necessarily be moved to go out and purchase a CD. By the time you hear it the seventh time, the odds of you remembering the song, singing a lyric from the song, or even purchasing the CD have increased dramatically. That's why major record labels dish out major cash for repetitive airplay. That's also why you find yourself singing the lyrics of songs you don't even like. The more you hear it, the more the odds increase that you'll act on the song in some form or fashion.

I'm still singing the words of "She Drives Me Crazy" by The Fine Young Cannibals from the late '80s, *and I can't stand that song!* How sick is that?

During the drama of my business and personal collapse, I often found myself surrounded by people who verified just how bad things were. These people were the noise.

Even more, in the first part of the drama, I started watching endless hours of television, looking for some type of mindless escape from what was happening. If you've looked at television lately, you know it doesn't provide escape – it just verifies your worst fears. I made a personal decision not to watch television for three months. This end to watching television made a huge difference in freeing up more time in my life, making me more contemplative and reflective, helping me to be more engaging in conversations, and allowing me to find friends who offered a more positive approach to crises in general. You may want to consider this approach, too.

WHAT TO DO NOW

It's spring-cleaning time! You absolutely must go through your house, car, and workplace, and dump anything that works against who you believe you are or where you really want to be in life. This is for keeps, so you have to be ruthless with yourself in this process.

Not watching television for three months can be the most revolutionary thing you do in your life. It will absolutely turn your world upside down. Not watching television for three months is an undertaking for only the brave and committed. You will see dramatic results.

For those of you who find it tough to break away from the tube, let me make this suggestion. Create a television schedule. Plan what you will watch. Don't channel surf looking for something interesting. Plan one day of the week where you don't watch or listen to any television, movies, or radio stations at all. Do this for three months. Fill that time during the 90 days with writing in your journal and/or prayer and meditation. After 90 days, you'll find that you don't miss mass media as much as you thought you would. After this period, add another non-media day.

CHAPTER SEVEN

CHANGE THE WAY YOU TELL YOUR LIFE'S STORY TO A HERO'S STORY.

Many of the homeless students saw themselves as guilty. Guilty of mistakes, guilty of failure, guilty of not living life the way they thought they should. The problem with that thinking is that it has this powerful ability to absolutely immobilize the mind and destroy the soul over an extended period of time. There is no honor, reward, or redemption in guilt, but yet, so many people choose it as a way of handling some of life's situations. When my students would go there, I would tell them about the hero's journey.

The story of the hero is the oldest and the most consistent story throughout the world. The hero's story is always the same – departure, conflict, empowerment, return. A book that grabbed me by the arm and wouldn't let me go was one called *Hero With The African Face* by Clyde Ford. In his book about ancient traditional African myths, evidence of these four movements in the hero's adventure is uncovered in almost all ancient African hero stories – humanity's first stories. In these mythical journeys, the heroes aid us in navigating this trek called life by helping us to find strength and courage where we thought we had none, by helping us venture deeply within ourselves where we thought there was nothing to venture into, and by awakening our greater selves where we thought only the devil existed.

Randy was a stocky, well-groomed young guy from Indiana who ended up homeless because of some bad breaks he experienced upon being fired from his security job. The tough times led him back to the evangelical church that he had grown up in, to rededicate his life to Christ. Unfortunately, he also rededicated his life to the idea of guilt. In one of our discussions, he told the class that everyone was a sinner and needed to repent in order to break the cycle of homelessness. He often went into great detail, sometimes offering us TMI (too much information), describing some of the very personal scandals surrounding his life. "If you don't turn to Jesus, all of the stuff you did will make your life a failure and even worse, you'll end up in hell."

In a very real way, he was using guilt and fear as a weapon in an attempt to get people to believe as he does.

My personal experience is that God doesn't need fear and guilt to make us believe. Love is enough. It seemed more Mafioso-like than God-like to scare folks into doing the right thing. In fact, Randy's discussion reminded me very much of the third-grade bully who used to rob me of my lunch money.

Well, to be fair, he never really did the work. His flunkies did the dirty work. They would come to me, drop his name in the conversation, and let me know, in very clear terms, that if I didn't give them my lunch money, he, the bully, would come after me. Being the 68-pound weakling that I was then, I was more than happy to hand over the loot for the promise of seeing tomorrow without a fist in my face. To this day, I still don't know if the bully really issued those warnings to me or if the flunkies were just freelancing.

Coming from that place, I felt a need to modify Randy's statement. I told him and the class that the adventures and misadventures all of us have in life are part of our life's path that make us who we are today. The salvation Randy speaks of is there for all of us, but only if we embrace, rather than shun, the parts of our lives that we don't like. Like the hero in the journey, those previous events have brought us to this point of crisis. If we are conscious, it will take us even further, to empowerment, and then return, but to return greater than when we started. In a sense, everything that has happened to us is leading us to something greater, to be "born again," *but only if we see it.*

That's not to say there won't be events in our lives that we'll not like and perhaps deeply regret. It only means guilt should not be part of that thought process.

If you notice, people who deal out of guilt tend to repeat the behavior that brought them to guilt in the first place, because they only deal with the *symptoms* of the crisis. Those who are able to take the hero's journey *transform* what happened to them by dealing with the *source* of the crisis. My experience at the shelter gave me clear evidence of one fact: Homeless people will return to homelessness as long as they live in guilt, fear, and shame.

At first, Randy didn't quite like my reinterpretation of his statement, but he kept coming back, asking me to expand more on this thing called the hero's journey. I was more than pleased to.

From the story of Jesus, to the emergence of The Buddha, to Queen Hapshetsut, to Homer's Odyssey, and the autobiography of Malcolm X, the hero's journey is being told over and over – not just with folks we read about in *People Magazine*, or see on E: Hollywood's True Story, but in our lives and the lives of other people all around us, every day. Once we realize that heroes are people just like us, we can walk this journey of life more like an adventure, knowing that we are not the first nor will we be the last to face our challenges and have the opportunity to come through victoriously. These aren't removed stories to be worshiped from afar where they have no practical application in our lives. These are roadmaps of navigation – literal "how to" plans – guiding us through life and its many challenges.

That's why these stories are the same the world over and have lasted through millennia. The theme is the same because life is the same, from the beginning of time to the 21st century.

One of the most profound hero stories I ever heard was from a 28-year-old mother of three by the name of Sherri. After class one evening, she and I talked about what being a hero is really about. She told me that she's gone through a few things in life, but didn't feel that she deserved to be called a hero. I asked her to tell me her story. She agreed and she shared.

Sherri spent most of her childhood in foster homes because the state of Oklahoma felt she and her sisters wouldn't be safe living at home with their mother. Their mother battled various forms of mental illnesses and used physical abuse on her children as a way to exorcise her demons. While Sherri remembers a lot of the abuse from her earlier childhood, she pointed to age 12 as being a turning point in her young life. While staying with foster parents, she remembers being taken to juvenile court for shoplifting and fighting in school. She remembers smoking marijuana by age 13, using the high as a quick escape tool. She remembers really branching into heavy drinking by age 14. She also remembers the day when her foster parents told her that she was going back to live with her mother because her mother had made some progress in treatment. A partial peace existed between her and her mom for about a year.

Then, mom returned to her abusive ways right about the time she turned 16. A few weeks after she turned 16, Sherri was raped. She wept openly as she talked in great detail of the rape, and how she cried for weeks after it, not telling anyone else what happened. Sherri mentioned how she hated the experience of always feeling vulnerable to someone, and decided that she would join one of the gangs in the city. She said that for about a year, the gang gave her a sense of protection and belonging – two things she had hardly experienced in her life up to that point.

After she was picked up by the police for pushing drugs for the gang, she was, again, sent away, this time to live with an aunt in Texas. Sherri mentioned that she connected with her aunt and stayed with her for about two years, until she turned 18. This was a relatively stable period in her life, but one that soon ended. Her aunt died of heart failure. At that point, she said her world came crashing down. "It seemed like just when I thought there was hope for me, it was taken away," she said. A month after her aunt died, Sherri tried to commit suicide. She took a combination of sleeping and pain pills with a hefty shot of Vodka. She spent three weeks in the hospital and another three in Psychiatric Patient Care. Once she was released from the hospital, she was able to find work at a McDonalds. There, she met a man by the name of Sam. She and Sam dated extensively. She fell in love. They had a child when she was 19 and were married the following year.

Two other children followed, but the relationship was a difficult one. Sam eventually ended up going to prison for selling drugs. She mentioned that after Sam went away, thoughts of suicide came daily for her. She left her children with her sister in an attempt to find work in Denver. Things were not going well at all. She ended up sleeping on several bus benches and eating crackers an older woman gave her. Eventually, she ended up at the shelter. During this time, she was being consumed by negative thoughts and depression, but felt she needed to do something. When she came to my class, she was one of the students who took volumes and volumes of notes, especially during the series we shared on loving yourself first. She said that for the first time, she felt hope about her life and what she could accomplish.

I realized listening to her that the job of the teacher or facilitator is not to get in the way of the student's thoughts, but to support where the student is. Allow them to get what they need at the moment they need it, and then step out of the way so that they will do the work their path is leading them to. As much as I would have wanted to take away the pain Sherri had experienced, I knew I would only create more difficulty by getting in the way.

By the way, after Sherri told her story to me, she shared parts of it with the class. One woman was so moved by Sherri's story she made a complete about face in the troubled life she was leading.

You never know how your experience can lead to the blessing of someone else. I wax pretty poetically about walking the hero's journey. The truth is, it has been an uphill battle for me to personally see myself in a hero's light. According to my early logic, I had done enough damage in my lifetime to truly be classified a villain. My thinking was that if I were a true hero, I should have been able to save my business, my home, my marriage, and everything else. How can a hero claim victory with so much loss along the way?

As the ancient stories tell us, there must be some level of transformation that happens to the hero because of the journey. That is the only way the hero can return victoriously. If the hero remains the same, it was not a hero's journey, but one of many experiences that will eventually lead up to the hero's journey. Had the events not happened the way they did for me, I would have returned to the same stuff I was doing before, feeling that all I needed to do was work harder or become more diligent. Through my losses, I had to become "born again" or die. This central theme was a cornerstone in the stories being told by the homeless. Many of them knew that they were walking through a kind of change, but they didn't know what to call it, what to do with it, or how to process it. For many, it just seemed like a more extreme version of things that they had been experiencing. One day, I decided to get way out there and throw out something extreme into our conversation:

> Me: *You've all heard about the Jesus story, right?*
> Class: *Yes.*
> Me: *That story is your story, too. Not necessarily what Jesus did, but the example that was set.*
> Carlos: *Explain that.*
> Me: *It seems to me that if you see the Jesus story as your story, you'll know that your own transformation is possible, and you too can become something greater than what you were before you faced your great challenge, your Calvary, your dark night of the soul. If you see the*

*Jesus story as just a one-time event, the only hope you
have is to die and, if you're good, go to heaven. Maybe
Jesus was just leading by example, showing you what
was possible for you, too, right here – right now.*
Carlos: *That's pretty radical stuff, man.*
Me: *I'd say many of you in here are in pretty radical
situations.*

When I started reading more stories of heroes around
the world, there were some valuable insights I was able
to glean from their lives:

Heroes have periods of self-doubt. If you know of a
hero who didn't have doubts in his darkest hour, I'd love
to meet him. Doubt is not weakness. It is merely the
reality of a life in transformation.

Heroes are always transformed. Their life challenges
and encounters make them greater beings than when
they started. Before you run out to change the color of
your hair, buy that new sports car, or dump your spouse,
know this: Transformation isn't necessarily external. In
most ancient hero stories, the transformation is subtle
because it happens in the heart first.

Heroes are subject to the same human frailties that
we all are. Few people actually know Mother Teresa
almost died of tuberculosis while only 35 years old,
before she began her greatest work. Motivational speaker
Dr. Wayne Dyer made the bold proclamation that he
didn't "do" heart attacks. Yet less than two years after the
declaration, he suffered a stroke. He's fully recovered.
Jazz great John Coltrane was kicked out of Miles Davis'
band *twice* for his drug addiction. He kicked the habit and

went on to become one of the greatest figures in music the world has ever known.

After reading their stories, I discovered one consistent qualifier these heroes all shared: they were human. If that's the qualifier, you and I are in.

As tough and as difficult as your times may be, there's nothing boring or plain about you. You are writing a dramatic and powerful story that will inspire others in the same way Fannie Lou Hamer, Buckminster Fuller, and Caesar Chavez's stories have.

WHAT TO DO NOW

The most powerful and effective thing you can do right now is to create a journal. Write down your experiences and tell how you feel about them. This is not necessarily for the next great autobiography to be read by millions, but as a guide to help you through the next challenge that will come your way in life. This is your roadmap.

It's not for someone else. It's yours – uniquely tailored to your personality and experiences.

A journal can seem like drudgery to some. May I suggest making a computer journal? Create a CD journal and write in it before the rest of your day gets underway. Even if it's just a sentence or a paragraph or a page, write something down.

If a computer document seems like too much, take out a tape recorder and voice your experiences. Save the tapes in a secure place.

In this time of great distress, recording this information can be difficult, as all things are right now. But I can't think of anything more important than that you're recording this information. Remember, this is one of the most important times of your life. There is a lesson in these times for you. Not recording it can lead to you REPEATING this event, because you forgot the lessons.

I thought that might get your attention.

DRIVING THE POINT HOME – HURRICANE KATRINA

It started off as a Category 2 hurricane, killing several people in south Florida and damaging hundreds of homes. As it clipped that state, it went directly into the warm waters of the Gulf of Mexico, where it was born again. The weather guys were saying that once it reached the Gulf, it would gain strength. It did, but this time as a Cat 5 with a projected path toward the city of New Orleans. An evacuation had started, with city officials telling everyone to get out. It's not unusual for New Orleans residents to be told to evacuate their homes in light of an approaching hurricane, so residents knew the drill. As with every hurricane evacuation, there are those who stay behind with the idea that they'll ride this thing out. Then there are also those who stay behind because they simply can't afford to leave. They don't have the money; they don't have a car; they don't have a credit card to go check into a hotel; and they don't have kin in the area. Simply put, they are the have-nots. New Orleans had one of the largest populations of have-nots of all the major American cities. With a Cat 5 on the way, and thousands who aren't leaving, you have a recipe for disaster. And that's exactly what happened.

Hurricane Katrina slammed into the Gulf Coast as a Cat 4, narrowly missing a point-blank hit on the crescent city. However, the storm hurled a 20-foot wall of water over the Lake Pontchatrain levee. The levee broke. The city was flooded. Thousands were stranded, many died, and lives were changed.

One of those whose life was changed was a young lady by the name of Keisha – along with her mother, husband, and sister – who left New Orleans in the initial wave of evacuees. Keisha is a 30-something wife who talked with me about what happened to them, and even more importantly, about how she made peace with the ground of this disaster:

> *Me: When did you get out?*
>
> *Keisha: We were in the first wave of people who left. We did what we usually did when asked to evacuate. We went to Houston and got a hotel room to ride things out. It just seemed like the same old thing.*
>
> *Me: What happened when you heard the news about the levee break and the flooding?*
>
> *Keisha: I couldn't believe it. I started thinking about all those poor people who couldn't get out. I knew it was going to get bad.*

Me: What did you lose?

Keisha: Everything. I lost my home and my job. I can't access my bank account. My husband lost his job. My mother was in the hospital when the hurricane hit. We thought she had died when we couldn't make contact with her for days, but we later found out she was okay. It's something else to lose everything. I say all of that, but I also realize that we came out with the most important thing: We have our lives and each other.

Me: What does this mean for you now?

Keisha: We have to start over. I know I don't seem worried about that because I'm not. I have my faith in God that sustains me.

Me: I'm interested in how you interpret what's going on. Do you see this as a total disaster or as something else?

Keisha: It can't be a total disaster because it reminds me to have faith in God. This whole event has made me know the importance of having Jesus Christ as my Lord and Savior. What it has taught me is to realize that all of our material things are just that...things. Things come and they go. Katrina is just a reminder of how true that really is. Once we release our faith in things and start focusing on God, life is better.

Me: What are your plans?

Keisha: I really don't know. Right now we're living with my cousins, and I'm trying to find a way of getting to my bank account. That's about as far ahead as I've been able to think. We're still trying to make contact with friends and other family members. We don't know if they're living or dead. That's about it right now.

Me: If there were something you would have wanted to happen differently in the wake of the hurricane, what would it have been?

Keisha: Better communications. It seemed as though when communications broke down, people didn't know what to do. It's like they immediately jumped to conclusions about what was happening, because to them it was the end of the world as they knew it. No one or thing told them anything different. I know that when people don't know what's going on, they get scared, and they start making things up. The people who were shooting and committing the violence just seemed like people thinking this was the end of the world. They just went crazy. I really feel it was the failure of communications. No one could call; there was no television, radio, nothing.

Keisha's assessment of what happened is clear and direct. The experience she and thousands of others had can be evaluated several ways:

1. This is just bad luck for the people of the Gulf Coast.

2. New Orleans is the modern version of Sodom and Gomorrah, and God is cleaning house again.

3. This is payback to The United States for the bad karma it has put out in the world.

4. Global warming is creating bigger and nastier storms. This is just a prelude.

5. It's better not to live near the ocean.

All, some, one or none of those things may be true, but we can say with all assuredness human disasters and catastrophes are about as consistent in the human experience as eating and having babies. A casual look at life over the past 50 years can verify that.

It is the Katrina disaster that further deepens my assessment that the only consistent part of life is its ups and downs. Once we make peace with that reality, we start to look at it from Keisha's view – we must communicate, material things come and go, we have ourselves and each other, and our faith can show us divine love even in tragedy.

I offer much love and respect to those who passed in the Hurricane Katrina event. We can also honor their lives and their continuing spirit by gaining from the lessons left in their wake.

From there, peace can be made with any ground...even when it's muddy.

Adventures And Misadventures

I never want to give anyone the impression that working with the homeless, with the intention of breaking the cycle of the homeless thinking, is a walk in the park. On the contrary, there have been many difficult misadventures I've experienced in this process, both the humorous and the dangerous.

One such experience happened when I was just a few blocks from the homeless shelter, picking up a cup of coffee from a nearby convenience store. I remember walking out of the building and hearing three men swear and curse in a way that said a beat down was imminent. I started to walk slowly, listening intently and satisfying my voyeuristic curiosity of what happens right before a fight breaks out. The central theme of the bitter complaining between the three was something someone said and their opinions about it.

In making their point, the men used a creative and impressive collection of obscenities, peppered with occasional shouting and threats. I heard something about spirit and deeper understanding and what you believe will become true for you.

I was deeply impressed that these men were having a "conversation" about something other than a sports figure or asking "where is that 10 spot you owe me?" Then, I heard someone say, "That's what Chet said." Next, one of the men said, "I don't care what Chet said, I'll kick his butt, too." And then I realized these guys were talking about me! Note that I'm still listening around the corner, so they can't see me and I can't see them. I'm thinking that now the conversation was at the point where someone could get hurt, namely, me. I'm thinking that if I walked around that corner, it was on! But I had to go that way to reach my car.

With this in mind, I put down the coffee I had in my hand, tightened up my stomach muscles, got my "macho" on and decided to take the corner and make an assessment as to whether or not I could take these guys.

The conspirators were a tall, middle-aged, dark-skinned Black man; a middle-aged Native American Man; and a shorter, older white guy. As soon as they saw me, smiles broke out across their faces.

They were all members of my class! I asked them what all the arguing was about, and they explained that it was a simple disagreement over the idea that we had the power to change our lives by our thinking. After clearing up the matter and walking away, waving goodbye, I was stuck with two pressing thoughts. These gentlemen were in my class and having a street corner conversation over how we have to take some spiritual and personal responsibility for what we experience in this life. That was always a central key in my series with the class – own your stuff, then find better ways of managing it. The idea that three homeless men, sharing a 40-ounce between them, were talking about this level of existence was profound. That triggered my later thoughts that true transformation, especially in breaking the cycle of homelessness and poverty, was not just for the well-healed and those who could afford to go to an all-day workshop with someone who has a book on the *New York Times* bestseller list. It was for everyone. The foundation for change in their lives was set.

The other thought I had was that I felt I could have taken all three of them on in a fight and won. At least, that's what my ego told me.

Before my classes, I ask if anyone is on medication, and if they are not taking the medication at that point, for what reason. For the most part, everyone takes their meds. But one evening after the class, a young lady hung out waiting to talk to me. She seemed agitated, so I made my way through the others and asked her if she was okay. She smiled, looked at me with unblinking eyes and said, "I hope we'll be all right."

Me: I'm sorry, I don't know what you mean?
Young Lady: I hope we'll not let it happen.
Me: I'm sorry Miss, I don't understand.

Young Lady: I know you're trying to persuade me to be your woman, and I know you know there is dynamic sexual energy between us. But if we pray hard, we can walk away from this temptation. You do feel it, don't you?

Me: Ohhhhhkay. Well, I'll tell you what. Let's make doubly sure nothing happens. Let's make an agreement that we'll do everything we can to make sure nothing happens. We'll make a pact. Let's shake and agree that I am nowhere near going to be your boyfriend and you are nowhere near going to be my girlfriend. Agreed?

Young Lady: Yes, I agree. Thank you for being so responsive to God's will.

It's important to report those kinds of incidences early so that if things get weird, you warned the counselor or staff of events leading up to it. I was told that the young lady was off her meds that week and had exhibited a lot of extreme behavior. While I am not the biggest proponent of medicating mental illnesses, there are those who do require it because of chemical imbalances. She was one of those people. She came back the following week and apologized profusely. I reminded her that we all have stuff we're working on, and that it was all good, and that she should always consult with her doctor before changing her medication requirements. I would say at least one fourth of the class was under some sort of doctor supervision and/or medication. Some of their challenges were due to the trauma of becoming homeless, and others became homeless because of their mental state. It is important for a lay person as myself to always defer to the doctor and encourage the students to take advantage of the counseling support the shelter provides.

I always say that when you take a position, you force others to take a position on you. Ever since I started volunteering at the shelter, the volunteer coordinators started receiving a number of letters from students in the class. Fortunately, the overwhelming number of them not only approved of my class, they absolutely loved it. Their comments ranged from "life changing" to "profound" to "he's one of us." The flip side was that there were letters that voiced bitterness about my presence. Some of those comments included "doesn't know what it's like to be homeless" to "smart-aleck college boy" and "his classes are too long."

This may sound a bit conceited, but I've always enjoyed the fact that I had students who would keep coming to class week after week after week. To me, that meant that I must be succeeding as a communicator. This was not a required class, so for them to keep coming back meant that I was at least mildly entertaining and, hopefully, at most, sharing life-changing information. But there was one guy who opposed my presence so much, he actually started spreading rumors in the shelter that my class was a waste of time and that I didn't know what I was talking about.

One day, other members of the class pointed him out to me. My usual policy is never to respond to critics. That is the critic's opinion, for better or worse, and my job is to support him in whatever position he or she took. But this time I invited the young man to join me after class so that I could speak with him about his concerns and how I could be of help to him in his transition. He turned me down:

> *Young Man: Naw, man. I don't think so. You frontin'. You say you had all this stuff happened to you, but you wear a nice suit, lookin' all clean and what not. You don't know what it's like to catch some of this.*
>
> *Me: Of course, I'll never know what it's like to walk through what you did. But you'll never know my experience, either. But that's okay because all of our experiences are valid. If we're having the experiences, they are immediately valid. We don't have to judge them or qualify them through something or someone else. If you feel that my class is not worth coming to, I respect that, and I honor your position. But please, let other people judge for themselves. Grant them that experience.*
>
> *Young Man: I don't care what you say, and you need to stay the hell away from me.*

And then he walked away.

My ego would love to think that if I just used the right words and said the right things, I could talk anyone into a successful life. But the reality is that homeless people have faced situations some would consider unimaginable. Those experiences made some of my students unreachable. Nevertheless, I must continue to do what I do. If we allow ourselves to get overwhelmed by other people's anger or sadness, we, in effect, become ineffective. I did that in my first year of working at the shelter. I can remember giving my cell phone number to many of the students in the class, telling them to call me if they should feel they are at risk. That proved to be a disaster. I was receiving calls every day, late at night and early in the morning. The calls, for the most part, were legitimate cries for help, but this approach on my part made me a helpline. That was not, however, the reason I was there. I was at the shelter to help support an environment of transformation and to give people back to themselves so that they could do the work for themselves. Occasionally, there were situations where suicide was being contemplated.

There was a young lady by the name of Katie. She was in a terrible state of depression because of the abuse she had suffered at the hands of her former husband, which led to her becoming homeless. While she was seeing a psychologist, I felt it important to provide additional support by being accessible to her at any time. She was one of the people I gave my number to. Night after night I listened to her tell her story of abuse, and night after night I would make suggestions as to what she could now do. Then I started noticing something. No matter what I said as a suggestion to her, she regularly returned to her story. My opinion is that once we get locked into our story, that story is the way we define the rest of our lives. She could *hear* my suggestions, but she couldn't *listen* to them because they didn't line up with her story's facts. Besides, it was arrogant on my part to believe that my wisdom was greater than the wisdom she already had deep inside, once she learned to trust it. It was because of her story, I discovered that the most powerful thing we can ever do for anyone in the middle of transition is not to counter the story that they tell but, rather, create an environment where they would ask themselves the questions. As I've mentioned in the spiritual buddy part of this book, we cannot interfere with their process, but we can give them back to themselves and give them the confidence that they will make it through – or not. Sometimes people don't make it through. We have to make peace with that possibility as well.

I learned that lesson in earnest in one of my trips to South Africa. I was boarding Air Emirates for a quick stop in Dubai, when 17 orderly, clean-shaven Black men, dressed in green jumpsuits, red hats, and smiles boarded. I'm not sure about the rest of the passengers, but having these guys on the plane gave me a sense of security. They seemed ready for any situation. The leader of the group just happened to sit next to me. His name was Joshua.

> Me: *Excuse me, sir, what are you guys, a soccer team? A security firm?*
> Joshua: *We are contractors. We travel around the world searching for and defusing land mines. Right now, we're on our way to Afghanistan.*
> Me: *Where are you based?*
> Joshua: *We're all from Zimbabwe.*
> Me: *Your job is no joke. You must struggle with fear a lot.*
> Joshua: *It's no problem, man. No problem.*
> Me: *You mean, you're not scared you could lose your life?*
> Joshua: *God protects us. That's all we need to know. That gives us peace. You see, you could die walking across the*

street or sleeping in your bed at night. We don't struggle with that fear. We know that at the appointed time we will leave this earth. Until then, we will live.
Me: (silence)

It was at that moment I learned the power of making peace with death in order to fully live life.

In the late 1980s, Colorado was shocked with a horrible crime that shook even the hardest of hearts. A young elementary school girl was kidnapped, repeatedly raped, stabbed over and over, and dumped down the hole of an outhouse in the backcountry. Miraculously, the little girl survived. The man who committed the crime was arrested and sent to jail for the rest of his life.

If there was anyone who would seem to have an honorary right to be bitter at life for her challenges, it was she. Yet, earlier this year, I read a letter she submitted to the local newspaper that told an entirely different story. The young lady is in college now, and she is also a motivational speaker. In the letter to the newspaper, she said she held no bitterness or anger from that crime. Even more, she felt what happened to her led her to her life's work – empowering and uplifting other people.

If there is ever anyone who fits the bill of a hero, it is this young lady. She has not blocked out the tragedy in her childhood, nor has she demonized it. She decided to embrace the event and make it a part of whom she is. That is where true power comes from – embracing all of life and seeing it from the perch of angels.

In another trip to South Africa, I was honored by the University of Kwazulu-Natal with an invitation to conduct a multi-day workshop on Compassionate Leadership. While there, I met one of the most amazing people in my life. Her name was Mbeka. She was a school principle in a school district just outside Durban. She was a delightful, strong woman who literally sang almost all the time we were together. Her general warmth and open heart was typical of the people of South Africa – Zulu, Afrikaner, Indian, and Chinese. It is that warmth that keeps me coming back to the country. Mbeka came to the conference and said that I needed to see some of the conditions their school system faced. I accepted. We took the day and went to the shantytowns on Durban's outskirts and discovered one the most tragic and wretched conditions imaginable. Whole families were living in homes no bigger than most of our living rooms. Without infrastructure for plumbing, running water and toilets were luxuries no one enjoyed. Mbeka took me over to her school and surprised her class with my visit. As soon as I walked into the classroom, the children began singing, and singing in perfect harmony. I asked Mbeka why the children were singing? She said, "Because you are here." Even in a school with nowhere near any of the amenities schools in the States have, these children still found it in their hearts to sing a song.

As we were returning to the conference, I asked Mbeka more about her and her life. She told me a moving story of how she was gang raped by several of her male students just a few years ago. She talked about how she wanted to leave her work and die, then she came to realize that the reason the children did what they did was because they really didn't know who they really were. Her job is to help them know who they really are.

As soon as she finished telling me that story, she started singing again.

There is something to be said about people who are able to take a story many of us would find unimaginable and see it as something else. There is also something to be said about people who are able to sing. There is something healing in the power of song. Whether it is the tragedy of rape or living in poverty, having a song to sing seems to provide a kind of refuge and strength.

I was invited back to South Africa by the university the following year to do a similar leadership workshop as a resident guest lecturer. The students, ages 18 to 35, were from all over the continent – South Africa, Ghana, Zambia, Zimbabwe, Kenya; as well as from Bombay, India. My host was a young Xhosa woman by the name of Kinshasa. Whenever we talked, she spoke poetically about hope and understanding that life is to be lived and embraced. From her conversation, I knew she had no fear of death and saw life as a grand adventure. One of the classes we held dealt with the AIDS pandemic that was sweeping across Southern Africa. In that class, Kinshasa stood up and told the students that she had been diagnosed as HIV positive four years previous. We talked after the class and she still had the same delight and bravery in her voice. Apparently, being diagnosed as HIV positive made her rethink life and embrace it from a whole new place. To her, symbolically and literally, every moment counted. That is the only way to live.

I've talked to literally hundreds of people at the homeless shelter about their lives over the years. A few of them have made serious transitions. These people were consistent in telling me about a time in their lives when everything seemed to fail and all seemed lost. They told me my class actually made matters worse initially. One man described it as a "freefall," because I challenged all of their traditional concepts about how life works. They also talked about that breaking point where that "aha" moment clicked in and they finally made a foundational change in how they walked through the earth.

Their view of *everything* changed. Those people transitioned into their greater selves simply because they saw their moment as the window of opportunity at the right time in their lives. Everything happened as it should have. Those who saw their moment as bad luck are still crawling through life, hoping someone will come along and pick them up. They have the ability to walk, but they have to embrace the fall to make that happen.

What I do with my personal "falling downs" will determine if I am in league with the young lady who triumphed above her kidnapping, rape, and attempted murder, or just another bitter, angry, sad person, looking for someone to blame and seeking someplace to hide in shame and guilt. I'd like to think that I passed the test and that I have been able to offer my experience back to several-hundred homeless men and women in a way that is tangible, practical, and applicable.

The seven steps to success I outline in the preceding chapters truly came from listening to hundreds of stories of people who have seen life from a place many of us can only imagine. But I'd put serious money down that most of you could not only relate to the stories my homeless students shared in this book, but are applying the applications I've outlined.

You don't have to be homeless to use these steps – just human.

The tripped-out thing about this whole journey for me is that, unless you knew me before, you may miss the change.

I am still one of the biggest jazz lovers in the world. I love smoking an occasional cigar. Something about a smooth cigar, rolled in Ghana, is good to me. Yoga and meditation are still a regular part of my world. I really enjoy pro football, enlightened conversation, golf, world travel, dogs, and working out at the gym.

Many aspects of my external life have not changed. But, just as I have heard from many of my former students who have moved on to finding a home and stability, a change has happened within me – my heart has changed. Some who have been close to me say the change seems like it's on a cellular level. It feels like it. Here are some of those changes:

• I always ask the question: "How can I apply unconditional love in this situation?"

• I have a deeper appreciation for all of life just as it is, not for what I want it to be.

• I always ask: "When did I do this before, and when I did it, what did it feel like to me?"

There's more, but the point is that internal change has a way of seeping out into your everyday life. When change is internal, you don't need to have someone threaten or scare you into doing the "right" thing – *doing the right thing is a part of who you are.*

The many students in my class often testified that when change occurred within them, no beam of light came into their room. No loud voice from on high shouted to give them instruction. No burning bush appeared to them. In fact, they started speaking about their change as being rather ordinary – even boring! After they started applying the steps to success, the change was undeniable.

Of course, *all* the students couldn't go where I was leading. But those who could felt the impact pretty immediately. As I've mentioned before, it had little to do with me and everything to do with them and their new awakening to the good stuff, which was already working deep inside of them.

WHAT I LEARNED ABOUT HOMELESSNESS

While there are many things I learned *from* homeless people, a good number of people tend to ask me what have I learned *about* homeless people. This book would not be complete without that assessment. After years of observation, here are three conclusions I know for sure:

- **Homeless people tend to seek ways, consciously or unconsciously, of fulfilling what they and other people believe about them.** If they believe they are "bad" or shameful, and that idea is being supported by close family members or friends, they will seek ways, people, or circumstances that support this idea. Most of the time they don't even know they're doing it. They'll come into my class and say, "I don't know why I keep having bad luck." My experience has been that breaking this vicious cycle requires honesty about who they really are, ownership for what happened, and then showering them with the language of empowerment.

• **Maslow's pyramid of self-actualization is upside down.** My experience has been that few people come to self-actualization and to the path of enlightenment when they secure the basics of life – food, shelter, and companionship. After they obtain those things, there may be no incentive for them to go further. Homeless people, on the other hand, have none of those things. Yet, they have been the most receptive group of people toward information on transformative and self-actualization ideas of any group of people I've ever presented to. That's probably the reason why my class has been popular at the shelter – the students have nothing to lose.

• **Giving panhandlers money is not a good idea.** It eases the guilty conscious of the giver, thus keeping them from fully engaging in doing something about the homeless situation in a city. It also enables the panhandler to continue this as a lifestyle. There is no incentive for them to look for organized shelters or look for an alternative to begging. This wisdom came directly to me from the homeless.

• **There are three basic types of homeless people – each needing their own special attention – temporary, borderline, and chronic.** I usually identify members of my class along those lines after hearing their stories and listening to their core beliefs.

The "temporary" homeless are usually the ones devastated by catastrophic illness or job loss. They are primarily the middle class and the working poor. Their financial situation has been tenuous for some time, but they failed to prepare for the worse possible scenario. Truth is, few of us actually make that level of preparation, but we have enough resources to draw on to mitigate complete catastrophe. The temporary are not aware that they have those kinds of immediate resources, thus, my one-on-one approach is to get them to become more aware of those resources – even examine why they did not see those things as resources in the first place. In my opinion, this group will never become truly homeless because they know they are poor but not permanently homeless. My job as facilitator is to introduce them to being great, not because they're better than someone else, but great because they are. This opens the door to even more possibilities.

The "borderline" homeless (the group from which most of my students come) are people who have experienced homelessness over an extended period of time. Their homelessness may have also started with a job loss or a catastrophic illness, but then started to morph into a lifestyle. These people don't have the crucial social fabric that can keep them from slipping through. I often think about Harvard Professor Robert Putnam's book *Bowling Alone*. Putnam argues that many people in America are increasingly becoming disconnected from one another. I would add that the more disconnected my students are, the less access they have to necessary resources to help them manage their fiscal crisis. Many of these people are parolees, former substance abusers, domestic abusers, and people with manageable mental health issues. I see them slide down that slippery slope from discouragement to hopelessness. Their words are unfriendly, indifferent, and hostile. That level of hopelessness creates a foundation that now colors all   perspectives *and potential opportunities.* As I mentioned in another discussion, this category of people seeks to make these core beliefs true. My observation has been that the only way to break the cycle is to get them to ask fundamental questions about what they believe to be true.

The third group is the "chronic" homeless. Out of my class of 30, about 7 of these students will be in the chronically homeless category. They will be at the shelter for a few weeks; then they'll leave, making a conscience choice to seek the untethered life. It works for them on two different levels. Some would choose it as a way of life. Many others were not able to "fit in," due to mental instability. In my opinion, one of the most productive measures a city can take is to obtain a breakdown of how many of its homeless population are in the mentally unstable group and dedicate a proportional amount of resources to just them. While this group will never truly go away, making inroads with the other two groups can make this group much more manageable.

• **Homelessness is not caused by a lack of jobs or housing, but by unrealized expectations.** This is a pretty bold statement in light of the fact that many cities around the country are basing their campaigns to ending homelessness on providing more housing and jobs for homeless people. My observation has shown that emigrants (legal and otherwise) are able to come to this country and find jobs and create makeshift housing. That should mean that those opportunities are also available for the homeless. However, the variable that I've noticed from my conversations is that homeless people born in the U.S. have different life expectations than emigrants. For many homeless, particularly the temporary and borderline, not meeting societal expectations of a home and job is traumatizing to the point of obscuring possibilities. In the emigrant community, the same personal and societal pressures are simply not as intense, if they exist at all. Thus, there is no stigma or disconnect in finding and accepting low-paying, dangerous jobs and sometimes substandard housing as a launching pad to a better life. Our society has created certain expectations to it's citizenry through advertising and implied cultural philosophy.

Almost without exception, my temporary and borderline students seemed intimately stunned by their conditions and by not meeting those goals. They often talked of their life as a failure. Many of my students were shocked to the point of immobilization. I feel that's why the 7 Steps work in many cases. They provide a way of dealing with the shock of unrealized expectations in a methodic manner. When in a state of shock, people are looking for direction because they may not feel they can trust themselves anymore. My observation is that those going through these challenges are discovering they can't hold onto their old way of thinking. Since you are not your thoughts, you can change and expand those old thoughts and still trust yourself at the same time. Once the students greatly expanded the possibilities of life beyond their earlier expectations, life became more manageable and reasonable. Things that were not thought of before, now became part of the discussion.

• **Homeless people are a barometer of societal trends.** One of the most unique things I've discovered about homeless people is that they reflect the tipping point of society. I remember, when I first started volunteering at the shelter, several of the students were talking about some pretty heady books, including one called *The Davinci Code*. The following year, the book was huge, being cited as a pop culture juggernaut. This type of experience happened several times with things you'd think homeless people wouldn't even pay attention to. My speculation is that when an idea or thought reaches the ranks of the homeless, the idea has reached the tipping point or critical mass in a society. I saw this demonstrated over and over regarding many issues, from who was going to win the Presidential election to why Tom Cruise was going to marry again.

I decided that before I make a decision about something, I would find out what was happening among the homeless first, to see if my decision making squared with what they were hip to.

YEAH, BUT DOES IT REALLY WORK?

While this book points to anecdotal successes of those who have implemented one or all of these 7 Steps, my approach to this class is a bit different. I do not go into the class with the idea of creating visible measurable results immediately. If that happens, it's great, but this class is simply created to give the student a chance to reexamine the foundation of his belief system without judgment. I am of the belief that when people really take the time to look at what is serving them and what is not, their inner wisdom (the divine spark) will help them make a better assessment of whether or not they want to continue that belief.

As human rights activist Malcolm X once said, "When you change your belief system, you change your thought pattern. When you change your thought pattern, you change your behavior pattern. When you change your behavior pattern, you change your actions." This changeover does take time. It requires a level of work and commitment by the student that he may not have experienced in life before. If the student is willing, however, all things are possible.

For some of my students, the 7-step process introduced in this book was exactly what they needed right then, based on their circumstances.

For others, the discussion is just "too deep" right now. I've always felt that my job was to make the information on transformation as easy and as accessible as humanly possible, without taking away from the integrity of the information. The temptation of each facilitator is to get away from just providing the information (the process) and start to become fixated on measurements of success (the results).

If the facilitator or teacher starts to mesh the process with the results, he or she will seek ways of "getting the numbers up." Thus, the integrity of the process becomes compromised for the sake of getting better results. In my second year at the shelter, I *did* want good numbers and verifiable success stories so that I could show my colleagues that I was doing something successful. My experience has been that when I focus on seeking better results, I start to skew an answer here and there or modify the discussion to focus on achieving a demonstration that my approach works. This is the work of the runaway ego, and it has derailed many a good teacher – and almost derailed me. So the more I started paying attention to the students' stories – even the stories of those who came back to the homeless shelter after becoming homeless again – the more I started realizing that foundational changes were made by the students in their belief systems, even when those changes did not demonstrate themselves immediately. This is a different take on success that, I believe, is more effective in the end. Many years may pass before some students finally "get" a newly learned concept.

Chances are, they may not be ready at the time that it's first presented, but that does not mean that the information falls on deaf ears. The key for the facilitator/teacher is to put out the intention for the student to get the information, then release the outcome. This more long-term approach runs directly against our society's immediate-results culture. However, the long-term change is more permanent than the revolving door immediate results cycle that may be more designed to demonstrate the success of the doctors than that of the patients. The re-ordering of life based on the 7 principles I talk about in this book is no mean trick. The student will need time to contemplate, reflect, mediate, pray, and "marinate" over her life before the idea of making peace with the ground actually "kicks in."

PACK YOUR BAGS APPROPRIATELY

This book is about the homeless – and it's about all of us. All of us have walked or will walk through transitional moments of trauma or drama that require more from us than any other time in our lives.

It truly is the hero's journey of walking through the valley of the shadows. I have also observed that there are several things each of us must pack as we journey through those valleys. Here are the necessary items for your overnight kit.

1. Get yourself some of that yellow **"POLICE – DO NOT ENTER"** tape. Stick some of it on the front door of your room or around your house, just so that you can keep friends and family in check. You need time alone. Take it. Your place may look like a crime scene but, hey, that'll keep other people away.

2. Practice saying "It's All Good" when something weird happens in your life. This will remind you of the fact that good is in everything that happens to you.

3. Take a crowbar. Use it to pry the window of opportunity open when you're tempted to just look through it.

4. Remember those multicolored kaleidoscopes you could turn with your hands and see all the beautiful and wonderful designs? Pack one of those. It'll remind you that, just like turning the kaleidoscope, you must create your vision.

5. Take an extra shoe. This is to remind you that you have to have a spiritual witness or spiritual buddy to walk through this journey with you.

6. Pack a set of earplugs. This is to remind you to turn down the noise, turn off the junk, and find out what it's like to hear yourself think – in silence.

7. And pack a cape. Remember, you are the hero you've been waiting for. Walk your hero's journey.

I send you love and peace on your journey of a lifetime. Have a great "trip"!

HOW TO ENGAGE THE AUTHOR

Chet W. Sisk's sole purpose in life is to help people and organizations reinterpret trauma and drama, using it as a way to transform to a greater life. From Budapest, Hungary; to Durban, South Africa; Montreux, Switzerland; Paris, France; and Toronto, Canada, Chet has provided his world-class keynote presentations, talks, and workshops around the globe to business, leadership, and holistic living conferences. Drawing on his experience as a television news reporter, CEO of an advertising agency, a concert Double E-Flat French Horn player, father, and author, Chet dismantles the myths of life by simply telling the truth – how we interpret what's happening in our lives determines what life will become for us. Chet provides tools and techniques to implement this simple truth on a practical daily basis.

Find out more about Chet at www.ChetSisk.com

Chet can be booked through:

Brenda Fraser
Gala Force Events
118 North Second Street #207
St. Charles, MO 63301
636-410-0345 office
314-704-4412 cell
e-mail: galaforce@msn.com
web site: www.GalaForceEvents.com